PARDES RIMONIM

PARDES RIMONIM

A Manual for the Jewish Family

HARAV MOSHE DAVID TENDLER

Rosh Yeshiva, Yeshivas Rabbenu Yitzchak Elchanan
Rav, Kehillat Monsey, New York
Professor of Biology, Yeshiva College
Professor of Medical Ethics, Yeshiva University

KTAV PUBLISHING HOUSE, INC.
Hoboken • 1988

Library of Congress Cataloging-in-Publication Data

Tendler, Moshe David, 1926-
  Pardes rimonim.

  1. Purity, Ritual (Judaism)   2. Marriage — Religious aspects — Judaism.   I. Title.
BM702.T46 1988   296.3'85   88-1219
ISBN 0-88125-144-5

Manufactured in the United States of America

To my *talmidim* and *haverim*,
whose love of Torah and unstinting committment
to *halacha* and *Torah hashkofa* compelled me to fulfill the dictum

אל תגמגם ותאמר לו [קדושין ל.]

TABLE OF CONTENTS

BY WAY OF AN INTRODUCTION

מה שמועה שמע ובא ונתגייר?

ר' יהושע אומר מלחמת עמלק שמע...

ר' אלעזר המודעי אומר מתן תורה שמע ובא...

ור' אליעזר בן יעקב אומר קריעת ים סוף שמע ובא (מס' זבחים קיז.).

"What compelling event influenced the father-in-law of Moses to leave his own faith and join the Israel nation?"

Rav Yehoshua said: "The battle with Amalek."
(Exodus 17:8)

Rav Elazar Hamodai said: "The Torah presentation at Mount Sinai."
(Exodus 20:1)

Rav Eliezer ben Yacov said: "The splitting of the Red Sea."

(Talmud Zevachim 117a)

What motivates a man to change his life style? Yitro, High Priest to the leading idolatrous cults of his time, adviser to the Pharaohs of Egypt, forsakes the prestige and glory of his social status to join a nation of freed slaves in the desert of Sinai. He joins them in their quest of a new social order based on laws revealed to them by an Invisible God who created the Universe, yet is concerned with the day-to-day conduct of each man.

What precipitates such a total change in a man's thoughts and actions? What drives a mature, successful, respected member of society to reject his previous value system and accept a new set of truths by which to guide his daily life?

Three of our teachers record their insights into the psychodynamics of human behavior by analyzing the motivating influences on Yitro's momentous decision.

Rav Yehoshua stressed the impact of the Amalekite attack on this fundamentally ethical personality. Yitro suddenly realized that the existing social order condones purposeless evil. Society remained mute and unconcerned when Amalek attacked a

xi

defenseless people, cowered by the hardships of desert travel, still bewildered by their release from two hundred and ten years of debasing slavery — a threat to no one.

The Amalek attack symbolizes the potential for evil in all men. It reminded Yitro of the Amalek lurking in his own soul and compelled him to seek the value system of societies other than his own.

Rav Elazar cannot accept this analysis as adequate to explain Yitro's action. Realization that man has the potential to commit great evil, that life is not full of truth and beauty, does not precipitate constructive action. To the contrary! Such realization often paralyzes man's mind and heart and may lead to the acceptance of the beast that is man as a fact of natural law. In all societies in all times, there were "drop-outs" whose conclusion that society is sick with incurable social and ethical ills convinced them that ambition was senseless, strivings and yearnings were but vain dreams. The gratifications of the moment became their goal. The reach of man was reduced to his grasp.

Only the conviction that there is a better way of life initiates the discontent preliminary to constructive action. Only the knowledge of Matan Torah, the awareness that there does exist a moral code that sets the tone for a life style uniquely suited to the human experience, convinced Yitro to break with his past and set out for the desert and a new life.

Rav Eliezer ben Yacov finds both analyses of his colleagues inadequate. Since man formed social units with codes of conduct, he was aware of the virtues of other social systems. Habituation chains man to the status quo. Family and friends stifle the faint call for help occasionally heard from the deep recesses of the soul. Even the full realization that this social order is inferior to some other system is usually insufficient stimulus for the requisite act of personal heroism — the rejection of the past in favor of a new unknown life style.

The great miracle of the Israelites' crossing of the Red Sea convinced Yitro that a Torah life was his only hope for survival as a human. The muck of the social morass — the natural laws of his society — was sucking him down into the depth of personal debasement and degradation when he heard the wondrous report that natural law is in harmony with the principles of justice. Man is not at war with natural law from without, or with his instincts from within. A Torah law that meshes in harmonious relationship with natural law has been promulgated for all mankind.

The personal God and the god of nature are **One!**

Man's soul yearns for a life in which social laws are in harmony with nature, and personal conduct is in sympathetic resonance with biological needs and psychological and philosophical axioms. Torah law and Jewish customs and mores offer such a patterned life style. A Torah life represses the potential for evil while directing man toward the fullest realization of a richly rewarding and meaningful family and social life.

To some of the readers of this presentation of the Torah lifestyle in matters sexual, there will be a call to courageously break with past conduct so as to enrich the present and guarantee the future. If this call is in sympathetic resonance with the faint inner voice that reminds each man of his magnificent heritage, then heed this call. Obey the voice from within. It is the same voice heard by our fathers at the foot of Mount Sinai ... "If you but heed my voice and observe my Covenant, you shall be unto me a chosen people ... a holy nation." *(Exodus 19:15)*

PREFACE TO THE THIRD EDITION

מִשְׁפְּטֵי ד' אמת צדקו יחדיו [תהלים יט; י]

The ordinances of our God are true;
they are righteous when viewed in totality.
Psalms 19:10

Truth is an absolute concept. Righteousness is as perceived by the fallible, finite human mind. Often a particular Torah law escapes our rational comprehension; it is nevertheless true and valid for all time. When our Torah life style is viewed in its totality, the "rightness," or feasibility and sense of propriety becomes obvious to the sensitive observer.

Since the last edition of this work, the advances in the biomedical sciences have presented new problems of morals and ethics; issues which challenge us to define more precisely the most fundamental axioms of our society. These include the question of defining the criteria assessing the humanity of a fetus; criteria for determining the end of human life; when to treat or not to treat the terminally ill; new methods of infertility management; new formulations of the evolutionary theory; the impact of genetic manipulation on the world food supply and on the integrity of humanity's genetic pool.

In addition, the ever rising increase in the rate of assimilation and intermarriage, ignorance of the "righteousness" of our life style, and increasing geographic distance of Jewish communities from the centers of Torah scholarship, has increased the threat to Jewish survival and integrity.

This edition of *Pardes Rimonim* begins to address these issues by attempting to present the Torah life style as a totality, both conceptually and in practice. The new section on gynecological procedures, and the articles included in the section entitled "Purity of Heart and Mind" present the laws of family purity as part of the "righteousness" of the Torah way of life.

Moshe D. Tendler

Pardes Rimonim — The Pomegranate Orchard

"Your progeny shall be like a pomegranate orchard"
(Songs of Songs 4:13)

"Your children shall be full of wisdom as a pomegranate
is full of seeds"
(Interpretation of Metzudas David)

PART I

Family Purity

I. WHY THE LAWS OF NIDUS? HUMAN REASONS FOR DIVINE PRECEPTS

The nidus laws establish the following procedure: Marital relations are interrupted at the first onset of menstruation. After the total cessation of any menstrual bleeding, as ascertained by an internal examination, *seven preparatory days* must pass during which time there iş no evidence of bleeding. At the end of the seventh day of preparation, the wife immerses herself in a ritually approved pool of water, the mikveh, and may then resume marital relations with her husband.

A) Divine imperative.

These laws were promulgated by God and applied and enforced by our Rabbinic Sages. No better reason for Jewish observance of these laws may be found than the above historical fact. Their acceptance by the Jew, from the time he stood at Mount Sinai until the present, is but the acceptance of an imperial decree issued by the King of Kings whose authority and dominion we readily accept.

Throughout our wondrously complex history, these laws have taught all our generations the truths about the proper role of man's sexuality in his family relationships. The marital act involves complex psychological facets of the personality. Emotions of love, ego, shame, pleasure, and responsibility merge to become one behavioral pattern. Many fail to maintain the proper balance between these psychological forces, and thus degrade this most intimate human experience. The nidus laws, in their totality, present a life style that is uniquely Jewish. The nation which "chose to be chosen" as the nation of God, contracted with God to so conduct family life. No further explanation is needed for this conduct. It is our Divine law, our social mores, our life style.

3

But the Jew is required to question and probe the intent of the Divine intelligence. The study of Torah is the most honored activity for a Jew. During the preparation for receiving Torah at Mount Sinai, the Jewish nation declared, and declared once again *(Exodus 19:8—24:3)* its willingness to "do all that God commands." But only when they declared, "We shall observe and understand (the will of God) *(Exodus 24:3)* did Moses receive the Divine command to complete the eternal covenant between the Jewish nation and the Creator of the universe. This contractual relationship commits us to observe Torah laws because of their Authorship and, in addition, to do all we can to understand the truths, beauty, and utility of these rules of human conduct.

All of God's commandments have reasons. All are for man's benefit. None are arbitrary. However, the human mind, with its finite capacity and with limited time allotted to study, is an inadequate instrument for probing the Divine mind. Objective humility must accompany this search.

A mind easily confused by the symbolism of chemical equations, awed by the mysteries of molecular biology, and overwhelmed by the complexities of nuclear physics, must approach this search with timid hesitancy.

The best we can offer are human insights. If these insights add to the appreciation of the Godly precept, then the effort has been rewarded.

If these reasons fail to increase understanding and appreciation, this reflects the personal failure of the human investigator and does not impugn to any degree the validity and integrity of the Torah law.

B) Strengthening the emotional bond.

Rav Meir taught us, "Why did the Torah require seven preparatory days? Because excessive intimacy breeds contempt; therefore, the Torah ordained, separate for seven days so that she shall be beloved as the day she stood under the bridal canopy."[1]

1. Talmud: Nida 32a.

The marital act is not to be degraded to a physical act devoid of the emotional bonds and sense of familial obligation and responsibility. Sex, as an act of momentary pleasure outside of its full unfolding in the family context, does not befit human dignity.

C) Dignity and respect.

"Since it is God's intent that man shall love his wife as himself and respect her more than himself, to protect her and be kind to her as a man relates to one of his own limbs, and likewise she is to love him in return, and serve his needs, therefore did God ordain the laws of nidus. They teach man that he has obligations and responsibilities that have been commanded by God who gave him this great gift, and therefore demands of him proper conduct in accord with His Will."[2]

By emphasizing that the marital act is part of man's responsibility to his wife, the dignity of the wife is enhanced and preserved. Even the amoral, liberal sex attitudes of modern society have not abolished the undercurrent of shame and degradation experienced by the female partner. The Divine approval given to the marital act, when it is preceded by conscious, thoughtful preparation in accord with Torah law, converts shame to modesty, degradation to contentment, and female to woman. The marriage vows are sanctified so that they do not deteriorate to the level of legalized prostitution so common among some strata of modern society. The nida laws take cognizance of the powerful sex drives and harness this force to strengthen family bonds. The commitment to these laws precludes the "chance alliance" so destructive to the cohesiveness of the family unit.

D) Moderation.

By teaching that these powerful yearnings are neither evil to be repressed or sublimated, nor may they be debased as

2. *Baalei Hanefesh L'HaRavad.*

mechanisms solely for hedonistic self-gratification, the great lesson of Judaism — the Golden Mean of moderation — becomes the fundamental principle for all human conduct. Thoughtful moderation is a means of accentuation!

E) Nida laws and health.

Many mitzvos have obvious health advantages for the Jew, although the health advantage is not the reason for the observance.

The Jew, proscribed from eating the flesh of the pig or the muscle of the clam or oyster, is less likely to contract trichinosis or salmonella infection. Proper cooking procedures, or the growing of shellfish and the raising of pigs in sterile, disease-free environments, in no way reduce the validity or severity of the prohibition. Any health advantage that accrues to the family observant of nida laws is to be viewed as the norm of a Torah-directed life — not the reason for such observance. This reservation is particularly significant since the science of medicine is in constant flux. Medical progress compels continual readjustment of the scientific base.

Within the limitations imposed by the relative truth of scientific investigation, a clear relationship can be discerned between the Jewish family life style and the strikingly low incidence of cervical cancer (cancer of the mouth of the uterus). Many students of the epidemiology and aetiology of cancer have been attracted to this phenomenon in the hope of gaining new insights into the genesis, treatment, and prevention of this disease.

For many years, the relative absence of this disease among Jewish women was attributed to the circumcision of her husband. The absence of a special irritant (smegma) found in the uncircumcised male was deemed sufficient to explain the statistical results. However, in 1967 a study of Moslem women who also cohabit only with circumcized males revealed the same incidence of cervical cancer as their Christian neighbors who do not practice circumcision. The varied racial backgrounds and physical characteristics of the Ashkenazi, Mizrachi, and Sephardi communities diminish any possibility that genetic or racial resistance to this disease is a significant factor. Indeed, tragic evidence is accumulating to indicate that the Jewess is fast losing her "superiority." During the last fifty years, the ratio of cervical cancer incidence among non-Jewesses and Jewesses dropped from approximately 20:1 to 5:1. Since the evidence of this disease in the general population has not changed significantly during this period, the evidence shows that there was a four-fold increase in the incidence of this disease among Jewish women.[3]

In a recent definitive study on the epidemiology of cervical cancer, evidence is presented that at certain times in the life of the woman the cervical lining is uniquely sensitive to the cancer-producing potential of human sperm. This is especially true in early adolescence and immediately after pregnancy.[4] The general pattern of the sex life of the Jew, with its prescribed abstinence after the birth of a child, its abhorrence of sexual promiscuity, and its lessons of moderation, is now considered the key factor in protecting the Jewess against cervical cancer.[4a] A leading investigator of this disease summarizes these statistical results as follows:

"The decreasing difference in incidence of cervical cancer between Jewess and Gentile may in some way be due to the liberalization of attitudes toward ancient religious laws with associated decline in observance."[5]

Intensive investigations of this phenomenon are still in progress. The hormonal and local effects of the marital act, as related to the stage of the menstrual cycle, are being studied. The conclusion, however is inescapable. Our way is a good way. It conforms to the Covenant between God and Israel. It leads to good health and a contented life.

3. K.T. Abu-Daoud. 1967 Cancer 20:1706.
4. M. Coppleson, 1969, British J. Hospital Med. p. 961–980.
4a. A. Baram and A. Schachter, The Lancet, Nov. 27, 1982, p. 747; R. Stein-Werblowsky, ibid., p. 1213; D. Skegg, P. Corwin, C. Paul, ibid., Sept. 11, 1982, pp. 581–583.
5. A. Singer et al 1968, Editorial, Med. J. Australia p. 1138.

II. THE BIOLOGY OF NIDUS

A) Anatomy and physiology of menstruation.

The menstrual cycle involves the interaction of many hormones as well as the central nervous system. A concise outline of the major influences on the menstrual cycle will aid in understanding the nida laws. The errorless transmission of Torah law from generation to generation often includes ancillary information essential to their comprehension. Our Sages were heir to scientific facts and concepts only recently ascertained. The Talmudic scholars knew that the female liberated an ovum (egg) that participated with the male sperm in the creation of the new individual. They knew of the presence and function of the Fallopian tubes hundreds of years before Fallopius lived, and they wrote with conviction of the psychosomatic and neural influences on the menstrual cycle. The biological facts were revealed to the Jewish nation when Moses taught them the nida laws so that, within the finite limits of human intelligence, the Jew could properly apply his mental faculties, this spark of Divine intelligence that is man's Godly image, to illuminate the pathways of his life.

Under the controlling influence of the pituitary gland, the ovary — really a dual gland — secrets two hormones, estrogen and progesterone. During the first half of the average 30-day cycle, the estrogen hormones influence the uterine lining (endomentrium) to proliferate rapidly and increase in vascularity and in glandular cells. At about the mid-point an egg follicle, which has been maturing, ruptures, liberating the egg (ovum) which is transported down the Fallopian tubes, there to await contact with a sperm cell and fertilization. The cells surrounding the ruptured egg follicle begin to function as a new gland and produce increasing quantities of the hormone, progesterone. This hormone prepares the uterine lining for pregnancy by inducing further cell growth, greater blood supply and glandular development. If the wife has been to

חתך אורך של הרחם והפרוזדור

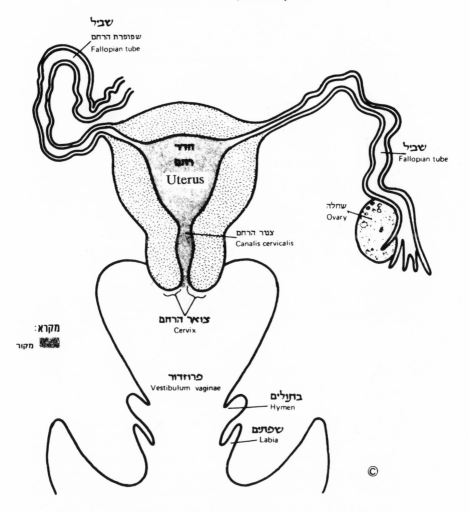

שביל
שפופרת הרחם
Fallopian tube

חדר רחם
Uterus

שביל
Fallopian tube

שחלה
Ovary

צטר הרחם
Canalis cervicalis

מקרא:
מקור

צואר הרחם
Cervix

פרוזדור
Vestibulum vaginae

בתולים
Hymen

שפתים
Labia

©

חתך אורך צידי של אגן הירכים של האשה

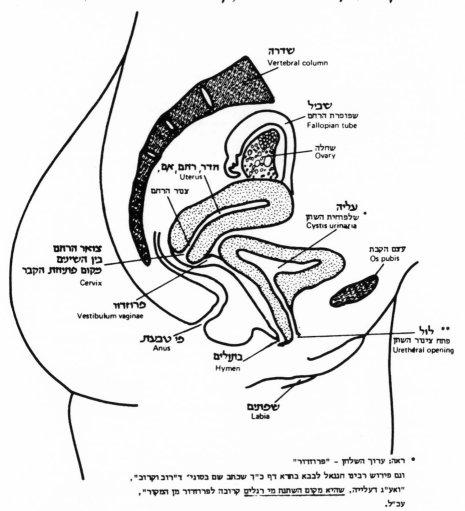

* ראה: ערוך השלחן – "פרוזדור"
ונם פירוש רביט חננאל לבבא בתרא דף כ"ד שכתב שם בסוגי' ד"רוב וקרוב",
"ראע"ג דעלייה, שהיא <u>מקום השתנת מי רגלים</u> קרובה לפרוזדור מן המקר",
עכ"ל.

** העליה <u>על גבי החדר</u> כאשר האשה שוכבת על גבה.

the mikveh after the seven preparatory days, she will cohabit with her husband at a time close to her fertile period (ovulation time). If pregnancy intervenes, the secretion of progesterone by this new ovarian gland (corpus luteum) is maintained and supplemented by pregnancy hormones from the developing placenta.

In the absence of pregnancy, there is a decline in both estrogen and progesterone hormone levels. The uterine lining blood vessels, deprived of the hormone supply necessary for their physiological integrity, become fragile and compressed. At first only the weaker walled vessels break, initiating menstruation or the nida state. Soon the majority of the proliferated blood vessels rupture, along with the glandular cells, and are removed from the body in the form of a menstrual flow that persists on the average of four or five days. Individual differences exist, of course, in the length of the whole cycle (menstruation to menstruation) in the length of the menstrual flow, as well as in the physiological and psychological impact of menstruation on other functions of the body.

B) Artificial cycles; hormone injections and pills.

Any interference with the natural supply of hormones disrupts the phases of the menstrual cycle. Various aberrations, some of which involve interference with the master control of the pituitary gland, result from the introduction of exogenous hormones. Ovulation, menstruation, length of cycle, or quantity and duration of menstrual flow may be modified or totally disrupted. The use of hormone pills to prevent ovulation — and thus avoid conception — is such a major disruption of the menstrual cycle. By maintaining an artificial supply of hormones, the pregnant state is simulated. Under this pseudo-pregnancy condition, neither ovulation nor menstruation occurs. When the hormone supply is withdrawn, withdrawal bleeding from uterine-lining blood vessels occurs just as in natural menstruation. Any fluctuation in the hormone blood levels can cause slight bleeding or "spotting." This intermenstrual bleeding poses a serious problem to the Jewess under hormonal therapy since this "spotting" is halachically identical with true nidus.

C) Family planning — a passing comment.

The use of any contraceptive technique must be evaluated on two standards:

1) Is it medically safe?
2) Is it otherwise halachically acceptable?

A technique that introduces health hazards for the wife or her unborn children is to be abhorred by all intelligent people. The Jew is faced with additional halachic sanctions opposing any action that endangers health. Techniques that do not present health hazards must be evaluated for halachic acceptability. Only the most competent Torah authority, whose piety, erudition and sensitivity to family and social problems are well established within the Torah community, can advise on the complex issue of family planning. In general, only the health requirements of the wife, both physical and psychological, can modify the halachic disapproval of all contraceptive techniques.

III. THE NIDA STATUS — A DEFINITION AND CLARIFICATION

Nidus refers to the halachic state induced by the awareness of a **bloody** discharge from the **uterus** into the **vaginal tract** due to the **physiological disruption** of the uterine lining blood vessels.

A) The nida state — a clarification.

1. Uterus

The womb, source of menstrual bleeding as well as the organ in which the unborn child (fetus) develops. The uterus encompasses the entire body of this muscular structure including the **cervix** or mouth of the womb. The nida state is not induced until the blood leaves the cervical canal and enters the vaginal tract. Menstrual bleeding from any part of the uterus, including the cervical canal, induces the nida state. Thus, even women who have undergone **hysterectomies,** or surgical removal of the uterus but not the ovaries, may be required to continue their observance of nida laws. The surgeon may prefer to leave the cervical canal relatively intact (this was particularly common until the last decade), removing only the body of the uterus. This residual uterine tissue, if it responds to cyclic fluctuations of the natural hormone levels, will cause slight "spotting" and thus induce the nida state, requiring the full observance of the seven preparatory days and mikveh immersion.

2. Blood

Any exudate or discharge, colored other than white or light yellow, may be blood. When mixed with other body secretions, exposed to air, or acted upon by many enzymes found in the vaginal tract, blood can assume many hues and shades. These may include various shades of black, gray, green, brown, pink and red. Similarly, the physical consistency of this exudate may vary from watery to dry clots.

The determination of the nida status of an exudate of doubtful color requires the ruling of a Torah scholar specially trained in this area of halacha. For some young women, such consultation is particularly disconcerting, although it should be less embarrassing than consultations with the obstetrician or gynecologist. If so desired, the tampon or article of clothing can be mailed to the rabbi's home with an identifying number on the package and an accompanying note recording:

  a) The day of the cycle on which the stain was noted.
  b) Whether the stain occurred before or after total cessation of menstruation was determined by internal examination with a tampon.
  c) Any special circumstances such as pregnancy, recent

birth, gynecological examination just prior to the discovery of the stain, or any medical problems.

A subsequent phone call to the rabbi will usually suffice to obtain a halachic ruling.

3. Physiological disruption

Nidus is induced by hormonal or neural mechanisms. The nida state is not induced by mechanical injury or even by an ulcer or erosion of the uterine wall not related to the hormonal flux of the menstrual cycle. A cervical erosion, with attendant spotting or staining, is a medical problem of halachic significance only because the definite end of the menstrual flow cannot easily be determined. As in all aberrations of the menstrual cycle or unusual bleeding, competent medical advice should be sought immediately. The halachic decision is often dependent on the factual information supplied by the physician.

A gynecological examination by a competent physician does not pose any halachic problems unless it entailed the insertion of an instrument into the cervical canal. In such an event, rarely a routine office procedure, rabbinic authority must be consulted. Any dilation of the cervix is considered to be an inducer of the nida state. The physician should be asked following an internal examination, if he had indeed passed any instrument into the cervical canal. The exact description and diameter of the instrument should be recorded for transmittal to the rabbi for halachic ruling.

4. Awareness

The actual moment the first menstrual exudate appears is marked by an **awareness** of this onset of physiological nidus bleeding. There may be mild uterine contractions, an awareness of some internal movement of fluid, or a similar subtle inner sensation. Most women are so preoccupied with daily chores, and so busily engaged in all the complexities of modern life, that they overlook these subtle physical signs.

Therefore, although **awareness** is an essential qualification in the definition of nidus, the nida state is not dependent on the presence of these symptoms. Instead, it is determined by the presence of the smallest drop of uterine blood found in the vaginal tract as the result of physiological uterine bleeding.

Menstruation, or nidus, is often accompanied by premenstrual symptoms. Often there are changes in breast tissue, muscular cramping, headaches, or vague malaise that can make the woman aware of the imminence of nidus. Careful attention to these signs and a determination of their accurate relationship to the exact day of the menstrual cycle is essential to the proper observance of the laws of nidus and greatly facilitate such observance. However, these symptoms are not factors in the definition of nidus.

B) Ovulatory or mid-cycle bleeding (mittleschmerzen).

Occasionally slight bleeding is noticed at about the mid-point of the average cycle. It may occur as a rare aberration in the menstrual cycle even after many years of menstruation. The gynecologists refer to this bleeding as **ovulatory bleeding** and differentiate it from "true" menstruation. It is induced by a sudden burst of hormones released by the ovaries at the time of ovulation and is halachically identical with "true" menstruation.

IV. THE NIDA LAWS — ORIGIN, DEVELOPMENT, AND CURRENT PRACTICE

A) Origin: Third Book of the Bible, Leviticus (Vayikra).

15:19 —   ...*If a woman shall have an exudate of blood within her body, for seven days shall she be separated.*

15:25-28 — ...*If the woman shall experience a flow of blood for many days, not at her usual menstrual time,*

	she shall be separated...until cessation of her flow. Then she shall count seven days after which she may (immerse herself in the mikveh and thus) end her days of separation.
18:5 —	*...Observe my statutes and judgments which man was entrusted to do, and you shall live through them.*
18:9 —	*...You are forbidden to sexually approach a woman during her period of separation.*
20:18 —	*...for if a man cohabits with a woman during her time of separation (nidus), and they have sexual relations then both shall be cut off from their people.*
12:2 —	*If a woman gives birth to a son, for seven days is she in the nida state.*
15:5 —	*And if she gives birth to a daughter, for fourteen days is she considered a nida.*

The above selection of verses establishes the basic definition of nidus and the severe penalty for transgression of these laws of Family Purity. The punishment of being "cut off from their people" is the same as that incurred for eating on Yom Kippur, refusal to circumcise a son, or eating *chametz* on Pesach.

The Torah concern with nidus is twofold:

— The status of the woman with regard to her marital life.
— Her status with regard to the special laws of holiness and purity associated with the Temple worship and the Priestly and Levite offerings.

The latter point has been the cause of much confusion and serious error. Since the destruction of the Temple, the laws associated with Temple worship have but infrequent application,[6] although they are assiduously studied in preparation

6. In Israel, the laws of purity and holiness still have practical application with respect to the modified priestly and Levite tithing and concerning the Temple Mount.

for the coming of the Messiah and the restoration of the Temple service.

The nida laws, as they concern this area of Temple service, have no force today. But this in no way affects the second facet of nidus. The nida laws, as they influence marital contact, have the same authority, validity, and sanctions as when they were accepted by our ancestors at the foot of Mount Sinai as the code of conduct for the Jewish family.

B) Development.

The biblical distinction between bleeding at the "usual time," requiring separation for seven days, and menstruation "not at usual time," requiring a separation of seven days **after** total cessation of menstruation, proved to be a source of error and confusion in the day-to-day observance of nida laws.[7] The need for clarification and simplification received rabbinic response in the form of a secondary or rabbinic development of the biblical law, so as to guarantee the accurate transmission of Torah knowledge and the meticulous observance of Torah law and custom.

With the biblical authority granted to the Sages of Israel, they abolished the distinction between menstruation at the usual time and at other times, and applied verse 15:28, necessitating the seven-day post-menstruation separation to all menstrual bleeding.

Rabbinic law always arises in response to the need of our people. It is ratified only when it proves to be useful in its goal of facilitating Torah observance.[8] It is in reality rabbinic law ratified by wide popular acceptance. Once so ratified, the law has biblical authority; and only under specific legalistic situations is rabbinic law differentiated from biblical law.

7. Even our great teachers are in doubt as to the definition of "usual time," with Maimonides maintaining a minority opinion that "usual time" is determined by the first menstruation at time of puberty, not by each onset of menstruation. (Rambam, Hilchot Isurei Biah 6:6) Menstruation "not at the usual time" is referred to as zava. Unlike nida (Verse 15:19), a zava must count seven days post-menstruation.

8. Talmud: Sanhedrin 37a.

The nida laws, as modified by our Sages, are now statutory.[9] They are not subject to revocation by any other rabbinic authority[10] nor is there need for such revocation. The acute insights of our Sages into the human personality and the social forces that mold individual action must be credited with the majestic accomplishment of preserving our Torah heritage as a viable and practical code of daily conduct despite thousands of years of relentless persecution, national dispersion, and intercultural friction.

C) Current practice.

The observance of nida laws requires careful study and continual review. This concise summary should serve but as an introduction to a more intensive program of study under the guidance of Torah scholars.

1. Definitions

a) *Bedika* — internal examination by careful swabbing of the vaginal tract with a cloth, or a cotton-wrapped finger.

b) *Mikveh* — a halachically approved body of water used for ritual immersion.

c) *Stain or Ketem* — a smudge of blood not observed during a bedika but discovered on white undergarments or bedsheets. The origin of this stain is uncertain since the usual associative symptoms of menstruation are absent.

d) *Tevila* — full immersion in a mikveh.

2. The onset of nidus

The "status quo" is a major force in Halacha, as in other legal systems. Similarly, the "usual" or "average" has legal significance. Until there is definitive evidence of change, the

9. Talmud Nida 66a and Brachot 31 a.
10. Sanhedrin 36a; Rambam, Mamrim 2:3.

"status quo" dominates. Thus, the halachic state of nidus persists until there is absolute proof that menstruation has ceased and that counting of the seven preparatory days was followed by proper immersion in an approved mikveh.

After resumption of marital relations, the non-nida state is assumed to persist until there is evidence of change. The "status quo" of non-nidus requires that evidence in the form of a bloody discharge be present so as to establish a new status of nidus.

The continually variable nature of the "status quo," the modifying potential of intervening pregnancy, menopause, or medical pathologies, combine to add new halachic complexities and nuances. These halachic considerations have been incorporated in the present day protocol observed by Torah-oriented families. The following summary is directed to the most usual and routine aspects of halachic application. Anyone presented with situations that differ from those here discussed is strongly urged to consult with halachic authorities for more detailed instructions.

The day of expected onset of menstruation is often readily predictable. The "biological clock" that controls the menstrual cycle functions according to rigid physiological laws. These cycles are usually of repetitive time intervals. Occasionally, the time interval is variable but instead there is a constant association with pre-menstrual symptoms or tensions. Sometimes the onset of nidus is consistently on the same day of the month. The "usual" or "average" expectation of nidus onset delimits the "status quo" of non-nidus operative previously and introduces the strong probability that a new nida "status quo" is about to be established. This probability is the reason for the prohibition against marital relations during the twelve-hour[11] period of the day or night of the expected onset of menstruation. At the end of this period marital relations may be resumed following a bedika to

11. Some authorities recommend a full 24 hour abstinence from marital relations.

ascertain the absence of even minimal menstrual bleeding. If the cycle is not sufficiently exact to predict onset of nidus during either day or night, then cohabitation is forbidden for the full twenty-four-hour period.

a) *The regular cycle*

A regular rhythm is confirmed by repetitive menstruation (three consecutive times) on the same day of the month, or at the same time interval between menstruations, or by a consistent association with particular pre-menstrual symptoms. A woman who has such a regular rhythm need not make any bedikos during the inter-menstrual days confident of the regularity of her nida cycle. If the expected nidus time passes without noticeable menstruation, a bedika is required prior to the resumption of marital relations.

b) *The semi-regular cycle*

Most women have a semi-regular cycle. They lack the absolute regularity of calendar date or time interval but can predict nidus onset within a span of a few days. For example, the menstrual cycle may vary from twenty-seven to thirty-two days. Until the end of the twenty-seventh day of her cycle she has the halachic status of a woman with a regular cycle and is exempt from all bedikos unless physical sensations suggesting nida onset are experienced. During the time interval of day twenty-eight to day thirty-two, her status quo of non-nidus is weakened by the empiric facts of the last few months. Therefore a bedika before engaging in marital relations is required from day twenty-eight until after day thirty-two. In addition, the dates of the last menstruation (calendar date and time interval) are also considered to be days of expected nida onset requiring the aforementioned period of separation. If a bedika after nightfall of day thirty-two confirms the absence of menstrual bleeding, no further bedikos need be made: It is acceptable *chumrah* to continue to make bedikos prior to marital relations until the reason for the delayed nidus is ascertained. It is assumed that some physiological inhibitor of menstruation has occurred (e.g., pregnancy).

c) *The irregular cycle*

Some women do not have any discernible menstrual cycle. The time interval may vary from two weeks to several months. Physical symptoms associated with nidus onset are also absent. Therefore, no one day of the month can be pinpointed as a day of significant expectation of nidus onset. Bedikos prior to marital relations are strongly recommended. However, there are three days which are to be considered as nida onset days with the attendant prohibitions. They are:

1) Day 30 of the last cycle which by Rabbinic decree is the average or normal expectation of nidus onset assigned to women with irregular cycles.
2) The Hebrew calendar date of the last onset of menstruation.
3) The time interval between the previous two menstrual cycles is also a determinant. When the same time interval is reached, there is an increased expectation of nidus with its attendant twelve to twenty-four hour abstinence from marital relations and the requirement of a bedika at the end of that day.

d) *The occasional irregularity*

If a woman with a regular cycle experiences an unusual cycle, there is the possibility that a new cycle is being established. The month following this aberrant cycle, she must consider as nida onset days, the following three days:

1) Expected menstruation.
2) Hebrew calendar date of the last onset of menstruation.
3) The last time interval between menstruations (i.e., the unusual one).

If this irregularity persists for three consecutive months the regular cycle is disrupted. The woman is then considered to be in the category of semi-regular cycles until a new cycle is established by three consecutive repetitions. The "old" days of expected nidus can be disregarded once the regularity has been disrupted unless the old cycle reappears. A single such reappearance reestablishes the original regular cycle until it is once again disrupted by three consecutive aberrant cycles. Once a new regular cycle is established, the old cycle is completely disregarded as a factor in nidus calculations.

The foregoing summary from which the more complicated circumstances were omitted so as not to confuse the reader, demands that every married person should keep a personal record of nidus cycles. This record should consist of the Hebrew month and date, time of nidus onset, and any associative pre-menstrual or menstrual symptoms. Whenever possible, a consultation with a Torah scholar should be arranged, to analyze this record after several months, and to review the relevant nida laws.

3. Determining the end of the menstrual flow

Sometime before sundown of the fifth day of the menstrual cycle, if a superficial examination suggests that all bleeding has ceased, a proper bedika is made. Without a bedika, the menstrual phase continues indefinitely. Intellectual proof, based on sound physiological principles, is insufficient evidence of cessation. Only direct observation by means of an internal examination can suffice. Except for special problem situations, such as ovulation occurring before the twelfth day of the cycle, the menstrual flow phase is presumed to exist until the end of day five. Assuming that, indeed, all bleeding ceases at an earlier time, rabbinic authority may permit earlier determination of the end of menstruation, in order to assist in resolving problems of infertility.

The bedika, which determines the end of menstruation and initiates the seven preparatory days, is the crucial evidence for altering the status of the wife from a forbidden partner to that of an approved or required partner. Careful attention to the following points is essential:

a) The white cloth or surgical cotton must be absolutely clean. Surgical cotton often has black spots intermingled with the fibers. These must be removed so as not to confuse the evidence of the bedika.

b) This bedika must be done before sundown if the following day is to count as the first of the preparatory days. If sundown is at 6 P.M., a bedika performed at 6:01 P.M. Sunday eve does not report the cessation of menstruation earlier than 6:01 P.M. At 6:01 1/2 the nida state remains unaltered so that Monday, which halachically begins at sundown, began as a day of nidus — if only for half a minute. The first full day that can initiate the count of preparatory days is Tuesday. If indeed the bedika was made only minutes after astronomical sundown, it would be advisable to consult a competent rabbinic authority.

Because of the critical evidence of this differential bedika, Jewish custom has established a double bedika. After carefully swabbing the entire inner surfaces of the vaginal canal with the cotton-wrapped finger and examining the swab for any evidence of blood, or colors that can be attributed to the breakdown products of blood, a fresh piece of cotton is placed as a tampon into the vaginal tract. Prepared tampons can be purchased for this purpose since they are used by many women instead of sanitary napkins to absorb the menstrual flow. These should also be examined for any colored spots prior to use. This tampon is left in place from just before sundown to true nightfall (approximately thirty minutes) after which it is removed and examined. Any questionable stain discovered during bedika, especially on this first differential or **hefsaik tahara** bedika, must be shown to a rabbinic authority for his halachic ruling.

The tampon bedika is not an absolute requirement. The internal examination by careful swabbing is **absolutely** required by Torah law. If it is unduly comfortable, or if such a tampon is itself a cause of staining or spotting in women with sensitive mucosa, it may be omitted or removed earlier than thirty minutes after insertion.

A douche, if medically approved, may be used prior to a bedika. A minimum of three hours must pass between douching and the bedika lest the presence of a small quantity of blood be not detected due to the douche water.

4. The seven preparatory days

Leviticus 15:28 states: "...Then shall she count seven days and then may she immerse herself in a mikveh."

The woman is in full charge of all the halachos governing nidus. The Torah has assigned both responsibility and authority to the woman. Onset of nidus, cessation of menstruation, observance of the seven preparatory days, and immersion in the mikveh are components of her responsibility and authority. Her statement of fact becomes Torah law. If she reports the onset of nidus, her husband is bound to conduct himself accordingly. If she reports fulfillment of all requirements for resumption of marital relations, her husband may respond accordingly. This power must not be misused. It is not to serve as a weapon in any interpersonal strife with her husband. If a wife states that she has noticed blood on the bedika, this must be a statement of fact, not of pique or tasteless levity. A later examination that the report was just to show her annoyance with her husband, and that in fact the bedika did indicate total cessation of menstruation cannot be accepted without the analysis and approval of rabbinic authority.

During the "seven days of counting," the woman should ascertain by means of bedika morning and evening that indeed menstruation has ended, not just ceased for a day. A "count" presumes a beginning number and an end number; hence, the bedika of day one and the bedika of day seven of the preparatory days assume critical significance. If the bedika of one of the intermediate days is omitted, the count is not interrupted. If the bedika of day one is omitted, the entire seven-day preparation may be jeopardized. If the twice daily bedikos prove difficult, rabbinic authority should be consulted concerning omitting the bedikos of days two to six.

In the event that no bedika was made (other than the differential bedika) until, for example, day four, then day four must be considered but day one of the preparatory days. Rabbinic authority should be consulted.

During these preparatory days, it is customary for the woman to wear white undergarments and to inspect them daily.

At the end of the seventh day, after nightfall (30-45 minutes after sundown) the woman may perform the tevila (mikveh immersion) and thus end her nida state. If necessary this time may be reduced to 20 minutes if her return home will be no earlier than 30-45 minutes after nightfall. Prior to this immersion, her biblical nida state, with its attendant prohibitions and severe penalty for transgression, is in full force. A bedika that confirms cessation of menstrual flow, even when reconfirmed fourteen times on seven consecutive days, does not end the nida state. The differential bedika, the seven-day preparation for mikveh, and the tevila, combine to remove the nida status. Omission of any of these components retains the nidus.

5. Conduct during the nida period

The blessing recited under the chupa (marriage canopy) refers to the couple both as "chasan v'kalah" (bride and groom) and as "rayim ahuvim," (loving friends). Praise and petition is offered to God for the sharp peaks of joy, love and happiness ("gila diza chedva, etc.") but also for the peacefulness and friendship ("shalom vrayus") that is to exist between bride and groom. A successful marriage demands both relationships. The "bride and groom" phase must mature to that of "friends in love." There must be contentment in the ebb as well as the flow of emotions.

Prior to tevila in the mikveh the conduct of husband and

wife must reflect the relationship of "loving friends" not of bride and groom. This relationship of "peacefulness and friendship" prepares the emotions for the fuller appreciation of the "joy and happiness" of the bride and groom relationship. All contact of sexual import must be avoided. All activities that hint at shared intimacies are to be suspended. Custom has established laws that modify the usual home behavior so as to acknowledge by deed the present temporary status of their marital relationship.

This relationship requires the formality of separate beds, avoidance of all physical contact, even during the day, modesty while preparing for bed or dressing, and a reminder at eating time that they are not at an intimate repast. The latter is accomplished by not sharing food or drink from the same utensil, and by an unobstrusive, private signal such as a candlestick moved from bureau top to table. Sitting close together should be avoided. The husband should not sit down on his wife's bed even in her absence, as evidence of her need for increased privacy. In case of illness requiring the personal ministrations of the husband, or vice versa, rabbinic advice should be sought for a protocol of conduct acceptable to the halacha.

6. Unusual circumstances

a) *Intermenstrual staining.* Blood stains discovered on undergarments or bed sheets induce nidus if they cannot be attributed to some external source. Whenever a stain is noticed, a bedika should immediately be made. Occasionally, rabbinic authority may modify this ruling if there is a problem of sporadic staining without any sensation or evidence of nidus onset. If the bedika proves negative, the stain must be shown to an halachic authority for his ruling. In general, a stain found on white undergarments, occupying an area larger than that of a 19mm diameter circle (approximately the size of a U.S.A. dime), induces the nida state unless there is a logical explanation that excludes physiological bleeding from the uterus. Of course, a blood stain discovered during bedika initiates the nida state regardless of its size. Stains discovered on a colored background are not considered halachically significant if they are not associated with the physical sensations of menstruation, and if a bedika proves negative.

If a stain is discovered sometime after tevila, when cohabitation is permissible, the full *minimum* nida period of twelve days must be observed. If such a stain is discovered during the seven preparatory days, prior to tevila when marital relations were still suspended by the halacha, the seven preparatory days are interrupted requiring a recounting of the seven days. However the initial five-day wait is omitted.

b) *Bleeding induced by the marital act*[12]

In rare cases the marital act itself can induce nidus. Any vaginal bleeding during or immediately after intercourse must be investigated by a competent gynecologist. His findings will serve as the basis for the halachic ruling by the rabbi. If it is determined that the blood was caused by mechanical injury or by microbial inflammation of the vaginal tract, there is minimal halachic significance (see paragraph c). However, if the bleeding is from the uterus, induced by the marital act, it can be most serious in its consequences and threatens the integrity of the marriage. The fullest cooperation of rabbi, physician, and patient is needed to resolve such a problem.

c) *Bleeding due to non-menstrual causes*

If a pathological condition develops, causing non-menstrual bleeding, marital relations are permitted until the onset of nidus period. At the end of the days of menstruation, it is necessary to differentiate menstrual from injury bleeding. Often this is a difficult task. If the

12. For specific laws of bridal night, see page 46.

source of injury bleeding is a specific spot on the vaginal wall, a repetitive bedika, showing the blood smear at the same point on the side of the tampon, may be significant. This evidence must be presented to the rabbi for his concurrence that, indeed, the bedika has established the end of menstruation. If the bleeding is due to a cervical erosion with blood stains appearing on the top of the tampon, not its side, a visual inspection by a gynecologist is essential. Careful swabbing of the entire area will reveal the focal point of the irritation and confirm the cessation of menstruation. The gynecologist must be sensitive to and sympathetic with the religious scruples of his patient. If at all possible, a gynecologist who is personally observant of nida laws, should be consulted preparatory to the rabbinic ruling.

V. MIKVEH

In most major cities there are mikvaot under the careful supervision of the local Orthodox rabbinate. If at all possible, only such a supervised mikveh should be used. The laws of mikveh are quite complex and are not well known even to the Torah-observant laity. Therefore, only rabbinic authorities, with special preparation in this halachic area, should be entrusted with the problems of building and maintaining an approved mikveh.

The fundamental laws of mikveh are here outlined for the guidance of the family situated temporarily at a great distance from an approved mikveh, who must use a natural body of water as a mikveh. It is also for the guidance of the laity who often, in the absence of a community rabbi, must assume some responsibility for the existing town mikveh. Contrary to popular belief, not every natural body of water meets the halachic requirements set for a mikveh.

A) The biblical prohibition against marital relations during the nidus period persists without any amelioration until after immersion in a halachically approved mikveh.[13] No substitute for mikveh is acceptable. Even if the woman scrupulously observes the differential bedika, the daily bedikos during the seven preparatory days, and then makes use of showers, douches, and baths, to assure all of her cleanliness, her nida state remains, with the full sanction of "being cut off from our people" if marital relations are resumed.

B) By Torah ordinance, a mikveh must hold a minimum volume of water, approximately twenty-four cubic feet. Tevila is of no effect if the mikveh water does not total this amount.

C) Since the mikveh is to be used for immersion by an average-sized adult, it must contain such a depth of water so as to enable full body immersion without undue contortion. The accepted minimum standard is for the water to reach eleven inches (28 cm) above the navel or waist line. An unusually tall adult will thus require a deeper mikveh.

D) The mikveh waters must accumulate by natural means. Water transported in containers and dumped into the empty mikveh pool cannot be used. The usual practice is to arrange cement channels on the exterior of the mikveh building to direct rain water into the main mikveh pool. From this pool, waters are supplied to the satellite mikveh or mikvaot. Once a mikveh has secured its full measure (40 "saah" or approximately 24 ft³) of water, it maintains its approved status even if transported or "drawn" water are added in great quantity. This halacha permits the central mikveh to supply any number of satellite mikvaot with halachically approved waters.

A portable tank, no matter how large, cannot — by biblical prohibition — serve as mikveh. Even if the waters accumulate by natural means, the fact that they are now in a man-made vessel disqualifies them. Hence, portable swimming pools, large tanks or drums, or passage through pipes and pumps disqualify even natural waters from serving as mikveh waters.

13. The term "mikveh" in its colloquial usage includes a natural spring or "mayan" even though their halachos do not coincide at all points (e.g., need for the waters to be stationary or non-flowing).

E) The waters in the mikveh pool must be stationary. If water flows out of the pool through outlet ports while the woman is immersing herself, her biblical nida status remains unchanged. Even if a properly built mikveh should develop a crack in the cement floor or sides, allowing for slow seepage of water out of the mikveh, the mikveh cannot be used until proper water-proofing repairs are made.

A "mayan" or natural spring whose waters come from underground sources is a most proper mikveh. Such a "mayan" differs from a mikveh in several halachic points. The most relevant to our discussion is the permissibility of non-stationary or flowing waters. Whether or not a stream or lake can be used as temporary mikveh-substitute, while traveling or on vacation, is largely dependent on two factual points:

1. Is there an outlet such as a sluice gate?
2. Is the stream or lake fed from run-off rain waters or does it have its main water supply from springs in the lake or river bed? Lakes or streams that dry out during the summer months (such as the many wadis in Israel) cannot be used during spring or winter months unless an area be enclosed with a dam to convert the flowing waters to a stationary mikveh. If, however, their major water supply is spring-fed, they may be properly used in the absence of a rabbinically supervised mikveh. An ocean may be used as a temporary substitute for a mikveh. However, the need for absolute privacy without the fear of unexpected interruption, poses a special problem with halachic consequences for those using outdoor mikveh substitutes.

VI. TEVILA

A) When:

Tevila is permitted only after nightfall[14] of the seventh preparatory day. Tevila should not be postponed even if the husband is out of town. Daytime tevila, even if after the

14. Generally 30 to 45 minutes after astronomical sunset.

seventh day, is not generally permitted. If the mikveh is in a remote location entailing a fearful trip after dark, rabbinic approval may be sought for permitting tevila during the daylight hours of day eight or later. Tevila on Friday or holiday evenings is permitted, but special attention must be given to avoid Sabbath or Yom Tov transgressions.

B) Where:

Tevila repeals the nida status only if performed in a halachically approved mikveh. Tevila is not a Divine edict to assure proper body hygiene. As evident from laws pertaining to preparations for tevila, the woman must be scrupulously clean **prior** to tevila. The need for mikveh remains a classic example of a Divine edict whose intent has yet to be understood by human intellects. The allegiance of the Jew to God and his Covenant is the only and best motivation for the careful observance of proper tevila all these thousands of years.

C) How:

1. Preparations for tevila

All foreign adhesion must be removed from the body before tevila. The entire body must be immersed at the same time. A partial or sequential tevila that includes the entire body in two or more stages is totally without value. Even if a single hair remains above water, the tevila is yet to be performed. Therefore, adhesions such as adhesive plaster, or water-repellent substances such as ointments invalidate the tevila.

Preparations for tevila involve three steps:

a. Biblically required visual and tactual examination of the entire body to assure the absence of any adhering substances.
b. The careful washing of those parts of the body especially subject to residue of sweat and dust. This later rabbinic

injunction includes the careful washing with water of all the hairy regions of the body, along with nose, ears, and mouth.

c. The careful brushing and combing of the hair.

These preparations should take place as close to tevila as possible. It is preferred that these preparations should be made before nightfall lest they be hurried and incomplete when the woman is rushing to return to her home. Special care must be used in preparing for tevila Friday evening. Since it is not permitted to comb the hair on the Sabbath in such a way as to guarantee full separation of each hair, or to bathe and shower with warm water and soap, the preparations must be made before Shabbos (even at home), and care taken not to expose oneself to dirt or soot on the way to tevila. This is particularly necessary when a two-day holiday is followed by Shabbos, and tevila is to be performed on Friday eve. The biblically required self-inspection assumes special import when the careful bathing and grooming occurred 48 hours ago. The intimate areas of the body should be washed with water prior to the tevila even though bathing of the whole body is not permitted, except for the tevila itself. A bath brush or plastic sponge attached to a wood or plastic handle may be used to facilitate this wash-up process since a wash cloth must not be used on Shabbos or holiday.

In actual practice, the procedures followed are:

1) After careful bathing with hot water and soap, hands and feet are manicured to remove all dirt, torn cuticles, and dried and loose skin. The nails are cut to a length that facilitates removal of all dirt. The acceptable length is flush with the fingertips. The long nails that occasionalaly become part of women's fashion should be avoided by the observant Jewess.

2) All cosmetics, jewelry, cotton plugs, and dentures, should be removed prior to tevila. Permanent dentures, or even temporary dentures or fillings that fit properly, do not interfere with the tevila. When a protective plastic cover is

used by a dentist during "gum" treatment rabbinic consultation is required.

3) Dried blood from a skin wound should be removed by
soaking in soapy hot water and gentle rubbing with a soft
cloth. Wound scabs that cannot so be removed generally
do not interfere with tevila. Rabbinic advice should be
sought.

4) Surgical implants, deep in the body and not visible from
the surface, do not present an halachic problem. If these
implants are visible (e.g., cardiac pacemaker), or if the
woman must avoid water entering the ear canal, the advice
of a recognized Torah scholar must be sought.

5) The body's excretory needs should be taken care of prior to
tevila.

6) Teeth should be carefully brushed and all food particles
that might be stuck between the teeth must be removed.
Custom dictates that, except for Shabbos and holiday
meals, meat should not be eaten the day before tevila to
avoid the problem of strongly adhering meat particles.

7) If available, a warm shower should conclude the preparation process, followed by careful combing and brushing of
the hair.

8) The final inspection by visual and tactile self-examination
is a biblical requirement. Special attention should be paid
to the removal of any loose hairs that fell during the
combing process. A large mirror facilitates this self-
inspection.

2. The tevila

Immediately after total immersion, while standing in the
mikveh pool, the "bracha" is recited acknowledging the
authority of Hashem who commanded us to observe the laws
of nida and mikveh. A second immersion is then performed.[15] An adult person should be present at tevila time to

---

15. This repetitive tevila is not a halachic necessity. It arose by custom as a
"hedge" on the problem of the proper time relationship between the blessing
and the tevila.

ascertain that, indeed, there was total immersion. If no such adult is present, it is recommended that the woman wear a loose net over her hair to guarantee that no hair had floated onto the surface, thus invalidating the tevila. A human hair net is preferred. The net should not have any elastic band that would prevent the entrance of the mikveh waters.

During immersion, the body should be maintained in a relaxed position with limbs slightly separated, eyes and lips gently closed. All unnatural contortions must be avoided, with the actual immersion occurring in a semi-squatting position with arms held away from the body. The floor of the mikveh should be tiled or cemented, and no mobile objects such a wood slats or mats should be used as floor coverings unless specific rabbinic approval is obtained.

Tevila is a private, intimate activity. Modesty demands that no one but the husband be aware when it is time for tevila. Wherever possible, the "traffic flow" into the mikveh should be so directed as to avoid any contact with others using the mikveh.

VII. THE BRIDE

A) Pre-nuptial mikveh.

A bride must observe the seven preparatory days after cessation of menstruation has been ascertained by the differential bedika. A virgin cannot make as thorough a bedika as a married woman, nevertheless she must make as good a bedika as possible. A bedika in depth should be made by use of a sterile cotton swab stick in addition to the bedika with the cloth-wrapped finger. Care should be used to avoid self-injury. The seven preparatory days should be counted as close to the wedding date as possible, with tevila occurring within four days of the wedding date. If the wedding is postponed for any reason, a second tevila, with its preparatory days, may be required. Rabbinic authority must be consulted. A bride may begin her count of the preparatory days immediately after menstruation ceases, as determined by a differential bedika.

The compulsory wait of five days does not apply to the bride, and she may go to the mikveh during the daylight hours of the seventh preparatory day if the wedding ceremony is after nightfall.

These are the only two modifications of the practice she will follow after her marriage.

B) Setting the wedding date and chupas nida.

The wedding date should be set as far as possible from the expected nida period. It is wise to expect some aberration, even in a regular menstrual cycle, due to the emotional stresses involved in the wedding preparations.

If the bride is a nida on the wedding night (chupas nida), the wedding ceremony is not modified in any way discernible to the onlooker.[16] They are not permitted to be alone, day or night, until the bride has completed her counting of the preparatory days and has performed tevila in an approved mikveh.

If the bride and groom do not return to a parental home until mikveh time, they must invite friends to join them. The halacha requires that "he sleep among the menfolk and she sleep with the womenfolk" until she can go to mikveh. Whereas, husband and wife need no supervision to guarantee their observance of nida laws, the halacha prescribes such supervision for bride and groom until the marriage can be consummated.

There is widespread use of hormonal regulators of the menstrual cycle to avoid "chupas nida." The wisdom of this practice is open to serious question in light of recent medical information about the dangers of exogenous hormone intake. Nevertheless, if a competent gynecologist-endocrinologist approves this short-term use of "the pill," it must not be taken during the last menstrual cycle prior to the wedding date. The

16. The "yichud" or seclusion of bride and groom in a closed room after the ceremony is omitted, but the guests are never onlookers of this part of the marriage ceremony.

tendency of the pill to cause staining or spotting, and thus induce the nida state, necessitates this ruling. Any regulation of the menstrual cycle must occur during the two or three months prior to the wedding day.

C) The bridal night and hymenal bleeding.

Our sages ordained that hymenal bleeding induced by the marital act should be considered as if it were a menstrual flow. They did not confuse hymenal bleeding with physiological menstruation, but sensed the need to issue this ordinance because of the severity of true menstruation induced by the marital act (viz. p. 36b).[17] Despite the onset of hymenal bleeding, the marriage may be consummated without concern for the appearance of this vaginal bleeding. Immediately thereafter, the conduct of husband and wife must be governed by the nida laws. As if to remind us that they were fully aware that the source of this bleeding is not that of menstrual bleeding, our Sages permitted the counting of the seven preparatory days after four days, instead of the usual minimum five-day wait. The total minimal nida period following hymenal bleeding is thus eleven days prior to tevila. If there is additional bleeding the second time, it is assumed that this, too, is residual hymenal bleeding, necessitating the eleven-day period (four days plus seven preparatory days). Such bleeding, even if it occurs many times, is not assumed to be menstrual bleeding caused by the marital act, with its serious consequences, until there was an act of intercourse free of any discomfort or bleeding. If bleeding recurs after this pause, it is assumed to be unrelated to the hymenal or injury bleeding, and necessitates immediate consultation with rabbinic authorities.

Usually a regular menstrual flow will occur soon after the first eleven-day "hymenal nidus" period, necessitating the full twelve-day minimum. This slow initiation of marital

17. Maimonides (Hilchot Isurei Biah 5:1819): "'Hymenal bleeding' is not nidus blood for it does not come from the uterus but is like the blood from an injury ... this hymenal bleeding is treated like the onset of nidus."

relations is uniquely part of the Jewish life style. The honeymoon period, so pleasantly described in secular fiction literature, is given an entirely different evaluation by the woman in discussion with her gynecologist or psychiatrist. The discomfort and unpleasantness associated with the excesses of the honeymoon are psychological traumas that blemish the marriage relationships for years. During the enforced abstinence, the minor injury heals fully, the emotional bond between bride and groom matures and strengthens to facilitate the new phase of husband-wife relationship.

Often the marriage is not fully consummated on the bridal night. The intimacy of the marital act requires a learning period. When both bride and groom are committed to the ethics and morals of Torah Judaism, it is expected that both will be experiencing this intimacy for the first time. The awkwardness of the bridal night is to be viewed as a mutual initiation into the marriage relationship that welds the couple, in their awkwardness, into an exclusive family unit.

In reference to this halacha, the marital act is defined as the full intromission of the male organ. If, out of concern and sensitivity for the minor discomfort of his wife, this full intromission has not occurred and there is no discernible bleeding, the nida state is not induced. If, however, full insertion did occur, even if there was no ejaculation of spermatic fluid into the vaginal tract, the eleven-day nida state is induced despite the absence of any discernible bleeding. If available, rabbinic consultation is recommended.

VIII. PREGNANCY

Pregnancy interrupts the menstural cycle. There is no need, therefore, to observe the laws governing the day of onset of nidus. This exemption begins after the third menstruation has been missed, or after three months of pregnancy — whichever comes first. Although laboratory tests may confirm pregnancy during the first month, the fact that some pregnant women persist in maintaining at least a stain of blood during the first few menstrual cycles, requires the observance of all nidal laws during the first three months.

During the later months of pregnancy, the physical attraction of the pregnant woman is lessened while her need for emotional support from her husband increases. The Mitzvas Ona, the duty of the husband to his wife, assumes particular significance during these months. In word and deed he must affirm the Torah concept of the role of the marital act in the preservation of the family unit, as well as the true mutuality of this physical activity. The need for intimacy in marriage is not exclusively the husband's prerogative. His needs are secondary to his responsibilities to his wife.

Any staining during pregnancy, unless it is determined to be from an erosion or injury in the vaginal tract, is true nidus necessitating the full twelve-day minimum nidus period and tevila.

If the gynecologist forbids bathing because of a threat of spontaneous abortion (miscarriage), thus also forbidding tevila, it is important to carefully explain to him the exact process of tevila: the temperature of the mikveh water, the posture of the woman during tevila, as well as the inconveniences of the nida state. Usually this explanation results in an early removal of the medical ban on tevila. In such cases, the preparations for tevila should be modified, with permission of a rabbinic authority, so as to substitute showering for bathing and body-temperature water for hot water.

Even if the marital act is forbidden for medical reasons, the nidus period should be ended by tevila as soon as feasible. The ancillary prohibitions which modify the conduct during the nidus period are in effect until tevila. If tevila be postponed until the medical prohibition against intercourse is removed, these ancillary prohibitions, if prolonged for several months, may become sources of friction and frustration.

IX. CHILDBIRTH AND THE NURSING PERIOD

The act of giving birth induces a special nidus state unrelated to the uterine bleeding. This special nidus extends for seven days after the birth of a son and fourteen days after the birth of a daughter. Since it is most unusual for a woman to stain for less than two weeks after childbirth, this special nidus has little practical application, except in some cases of caesarian delivery. In practice, childbirth should be treated as a nidus period. As soon as a differential bedika ascertains the cessation of all bleeding, the seven preparatory days are counted and tevila in a mikveh permits the resumption of marital relations.[18]

If pregnancy is interrupted by a spontaneous abortion (miscarriage) or by surgical intervention (caesarian), a competent rabbi should be consulted for the halachos governing this situation.

Until a new regular menstrual cycle be established, the woman after childbirth should presume that her previously established cycle persists. After resumption of menstruation (usually within three months after childbirth), the expected day of nidus onset is to be calculated according to the previous cycle.

During Talmudic times, resumption of menstruation was usually delayed as much as 24 months after onset of pregnancy. The then universal custom of breast feeding for two years served as an additional cause for inhibition of menstruation. Today, however, many nursing mothers begin normal menstruation within six months after delivery. The improved nutritional and health standards of our generation minimizes the physical rigors of pregnancy, childbirth, and lactation. The nursing mother, as well as the non-nursing mother, must therefore observe all nida laws, using her previous menstrual cycle as a basis for calculating the day of onset of nidus until a new cycle is established or the old one reconfirmed.

18. Some families observe a halachic custom of extending the nidus period to forty days after the birth of a son and eighty days after the birth of a daughter. Rabbinic advice should be sought to determine if this family custom must be followed or if the halachic procedure, outlined above, may be adopted.

Occasional staining during nursing may be due either to uterine contractions or to fluctuations in hormonal levels. Such fluctuations may occur as the infant begins to eat solid food and thereby reduces its dependency on its mother's milk. This staining is nidus, either way. If such staining should interfere excessively with normal marital relations, medical advice should be sought. Cervicitis may be responsible for the excessive occurrences.

It is important to emphasize that bedikos performed by a nursing mother must be performed as gently as possible. Attention should be paid to the softness of the bedika cloth and the slowness of movements during the internal examination. It is recommended that the bedika cloth be washed with warm tap water and patted dry with a clean towel prior to use.

X. NATURAL CHILDBIRTH — HUSBAND'S ROLE IN ACCORDANCE WITH HALACHA

Question:
Is a husband permitted to assist during natural childbirth (as in the Lamaze method)? When is the wife considered a *Nida* or a *yoledeth* (parturient woman)? Is the husband's role during natural childbirth an exemption from the usual *Nida laws* because of his contribution to his wife's physical and psychological welfare?

Answer:
Within certain guidelines (see below) the husband is permitted to be present during natural childbirth and to provide solace and comfort to his wife.

Comment:
The wife is considered a *Nida* or a *yoledeth* immediately upon the appearance of any blood (the "bloody show"; mucus plug tinged with blood) or any active bleeding from the cervical canal. She is also considered to be a *yoledeth* if there is no bleeding at all but labor has progressed to a point of:

(a) Contractions of such frequency and/or severity to make it very difficult to walk without assistance.

(b) The nurse or physicians report that the cervix is fully dilated.

Under the above conditions, the *Nida state* is established with all its halachic restrictions.

Prior to that time (i.e., during labor) if no blood appeared, the woman is not a *Nida* and may even have physical contact with her husband. When she becomes a *Nida*, however, as defined above, no further physical contact is permitted.

Although the hospital environment, the presence of the medical team members, and the preoccupation of both husband and wife with the birth process minimize the halachic concern lest physical contact lead to forbidden intimacies, it is *not permitted* for the husband to "wipe her face, or rub her back, or support her during contractions." Indeed, proper preparations for natural childbirth should include the husband's supportive role — but without physical contact. His presence, encouragement and reassurances are the sum total of his contributions. Any physical ministrations can better be performed by hospital personnel.

In the delivery room itself, the husband should not view the act of birth of the child but should stand near the head of the table and offer encouragement and reassurance to his wife. He should not even view the birth process through the mirrors present in most delivery rooms.

XI. GYNECOLOGICAL PROCEDURES: HALACHIC IMPORT

One of the areas of great confusion in the practice of Jewish family laws is the effect of routine gynecological examinations on the nida laws. As explained above, on pages 14-16, nidus is not induced by trauma or infectious processes. It is the bleeding induced by hormonal fluctuations, i.e., physiological conditions, that is considered tantamount to halachic menstruation. Thus, treatment with hormones of various conditions, such as infertility, chronic spotting, and neoplastic disease, may very well involve questions that must be posed to a rabbi for his decision. The spotting that may be induced by such treatment is generally classified as nidus. However, most gynecological office procedures, and a number of hospital interventions, are not physiological, but mechanical in nature; that is, there is no systemic effect of the procedure.

The main halachic concern rests on a principle that can be succinctly stated as: *Whenever there is a dilation of the cervical opening (os), the nida state is induced.* The halachic definition of dilation is: the stretching caused by an instrument or gloved finger that is passed through the cervical os if the instrument has a diameter of 0.7 inches or more. This size, according to the latest information, corresponds to the head-rump size of a fetus on day 40 of gestation.

A) Routine office procedures.

1. The Pap Smear

The Pap smear is now done routinely whenever a patient appears for any reason at her gynecologist's office, at least once a year. The Pap smear allows examination of a small amount of the material that is shed from the cervix, containing cells from the uterus and cervix. The microscopic examination of these cells can differentiate between normal and abnormal to detect the early signs of cancerous changes. The procedure involves the collection of a small amount of mucous by means of a cotton swab or a pipette, and the scraping of the cervical area with a blunt wooden or plastic applicator to obtain some representative cells. The size of the swab tip or the pipette (similar to a medicine dropper) is far less than .7 inches, so that, although it penetrates into the cervical opening, there is no halachic importance to this procedure. The scraping of the outside of the cervix may, indeed, cause a little bleeding, but it is simply mild trauma bleeding, unrelated to nidus. Since the doctor often uses a speculum to facilitate his access to the area, the pressure of the speculum may also sometimes cause bleeding or irritation. The minimum spotting induced can easily be differentiated from menstrual spotting. The Pap smear, therefore, may be done at any time of the menstrual cycle without impact on the religious behavior of the couple.

2. Cervical cautery

Occasionally a physician will treat an area of irritation on the outside of the cervix by electrical cautery, freezing, a laser beam, or cauterizing chemicals such as silver nitrate. If the area that is being treated is on the outside of the cervix, although bleeding will usually be induced, the rule that trauma bleeding is halachically inconsequential applies. This cauterization is often used to cure a case of cervicitis, or inflammation, or infection, so as to stop intermenstrual spotting.

This procedure should be done only after a woman has gone to the mikveh, since it is impossible to differentiate — without actual gynecological examination — between this significant trauma bleeding and the menstrual spotting induced by hormonal changes. During the seven preparatory days, the presence of any bleeding becomes problematic. In the event that this procedure must be undergone by a woman before going to the mikveh, a rabbi must be consulted.

3. The pelvic examination

The routine pelvic examination generally does not pose any halachic problems. Except when special procedures are undertaken, or during the last weeks of pregnancy, there is no penetration of the cervical opening. Any bleeding is due to the speculum and the rigors of the bi-manual examination. During the last weeks of pregnancy, however, the manual internal examination may indeed involve entering the cervical canal, thus inducing the nida state. If possible, this examination should be modified to be only a rectal examination that can also often provide the information the doctor seeks. The almost routine use of ultrasound also minimizes the need for this late pregnancy examination.

4. Endometrial biopsy

An endometrial biopsy is performed in an infertility evaluation (to determine if ovulation has occurred) or as part of the procedure to rule out cancer in cases of abnormal bleeding or staining. The endometrium, or inner lining of the uterus, is scraped with a hook-like instrument, and some of the tissue thus removed is stained and examined microscopically. Although bleeding will most likely ensue, the bleeding is due to mechanical injury. The scraping instrument is of very narrow diameter, generally not exceeding six mm (0.7 inches is approximately 17 1/2 mm).

5. Post-coital test

A post-coital test is done early in an infertility workup. This test involves removal of a small amount of mucous about the cervix shortly after a woman has had intercourse. For most accurate results, it is preferable that this test be performed the morning after the woman has gone to the mikveh, with intercourse having occurred early in the morning, so that the woman may be examined within two hours of the intercourse.

There is no halachic import to this test. An instrument resembling a tiny spoon is used to remove some of the fluid at the opening of the cervix for microscopic examination. Generally, no bleeding will occur unless the cervix is inflamed due to a prior condition.

It should be emphasized that the post-coital test must be undertaken before any rigorous testing of a woman's fertility is permitted. Too often the wife is subjected to highly invasive procedures to determine the cause of infertility before it is determined if her husband has viable sperm. The halachic complexity of obtaining a semen sample for early testing is the rationalization given for the above behavior. Indeed, especially in Hasidic circles, semen testing does present many halachic and emotional problems. The post-coital test, while not providing all answers, does give the main information needed: whether or not motile, morphologically normal sperm are present. Since this test is done on the ejaculate within the body of the wife, no halachic import can be attached to it.

B) Special procedures.

1. Colopscopy

When a very careful examination of the cervix is indicated, special magnifying instrumentation is used, and the cervical canal is usually entered. Since individual physicians modify this procedure, rabbinic advice must be sought. The rabbi will need a careful recording of the kind of instrument used and its diameter and a description of the manual examination performed.

2. Dilatation and curettage ("D 'n' C")

This procedure is far more invasive than those discussed above. Under anaesthesia, the cervical canal is dilated, and the inner lining of the uterus is scraped and removed. This procedure induces the state of nida.

3. Hydrosufflation, hydrotubation, tubal insufflation test

This procedure is often done in the treatment of infertility. It is a vigorous treatment to assure patent, physiologically active fallopian tubes. Water containing antibiotics is infused into the uterus and fallopian tubes. To prevent back flow, a cap or tenaculum is affixed to the cervix. This cap is the cause of any bleeding that occurs. The tube that enters the cervix is of narrow diameter and, hence, causes no dilation. This procedure does not induce nidus.

Note: The Rubin or tubal insufflation test, which is now used only rarely, is similar to the above test, except that a gas (carbon dioxide) is infused, rather than a water solution.

4. Hysterosalpinogram

A physician may occasionally order this procedure to obtain fluoroscopic and x-ray pictures of the uterine cavity and the fallopian tubes. A cap is placed over the cervix. A catheter tube runs through the cap to permit the introduction of a radio-opaque dye into the uterine cavity and fallopian tubes. Any bleeding is due to mechanical irritation of the cervical canal and is not considered nidus bleeding.

5. Endoscopy (laparoscopy, hysteroscopy, and culdoscopy)

This is an invasive surgical procedure that requires general anaesthetic. A small opening is made in the abdominal wall (and in the uterine wall in the case of hysteroscopy), and the field is examined visually. Biopsy material can be obtained. Bleeding to the outside rarely occurs. However, the physician must be asked if he or she plans to do any other procedure that involves dilation of the cervical os while the patient is under the anaesthesia.

Culdoscopy is an endoscopic procedure that has largely been replaced by laparoscopy. Unlike in laparoscopy, in culdoscopy the vaginal route is used, and careful consultation between physician and rabbi is necessary to evaluate the halachic consequences of this procedure.

XII. THE BRIS (CIRCUMCISION RITUAL)

A) The mitzva.

Circumcision is one of the fundamental acts of commitment that identifies the Jew as a servant of God. It is not merely a medical or surgical procedure designed to facilitate personal hygiene or to prevent neo-plastic disease. Indeed, as with all of the mitzvos, benefits accrue to those who observe the circumcision ritual that may have import in health and disease. The incidence of penile cancer is virtually unknown among Jews who observe this Covenant of the Faith. Similarly, the benefits of improved personal cleanliness result from this mitzva. Yet, these are not the reasons for the performance of this act of dedication.

During the last decade, the medical profession has launched many attacks on the almost universal practice of circumcision among nations of the Western hemisphere. The attacks minimize the health contribution of circumcision, with a clear undercurrent of subtle anti-Semitism, rebuking the educated masses for following the practice of the ancient Hebrews. The denial of health benefits is indeed scientifically untenable, but the attack is totally irrelevant to the ritual of circumcision which is, indeed, a private affair between God and His Nation Israel. It follows that the act of ritual circumcision must be fully governed by halacha.

B) The mohel.

The mohel must be a truly committed Jew, observant of all the laws of our Torah, and must be well-versed in the particulars of the laws governing the mitzva of circumcision. Included in these laws is the need for his consummate skill in performing this holy task. The mohel's knowledge of asepsis and his meticulous attention thereto; his mastery of the principles of hemostasis, and his specialized knowledge of the anatomy of the male organ, so essential in cases of major and minor malformations, such as hypospadia and chordee, are an essential part of the entire mitzva. Mohelim who are negligent in the performance of the technical aspects of the circumcision should not be assigned.

Since *mila* is a religious act, governmental regulations do not apply as they would to a medical practitioner. In selecting a mohel, advice must be sought from the local Orthodox rabbi who would be fully able to recommend those mohelim in his area who have earned the respect of the rabbinic and medical professions. Diligence in the selection of a mohel is particularly crucial when there is no mohel in the immediate area, and the mohel must be called in from another locale. The shortage of mohelim willing to travel to distant towns is often a reflection of the fact that the most respected mohelim are too busy to accept a call that will keep them away from their own immediate areas for a day or more. If mila is to occur on a Sabbath or holiday, the problem of traveling is compounded exponentially. The New York Mila Board, located in New York City, is the oldest and most active certifying body for mohelim in the world. The board can be consulted when it is difficult to find a proper mohel.

C) Forbidden methods of circumcision.

The gentlest and most efficient way to perform a circumcision is the way it has been done by Jews for the past 3,500 years. During the last 30 years, various surgical apparatuses have entered the field of surgical circumcision as performed by obstetricians and pediatricians, usually on day one to four after birth. These instruments are known as the GOMCO, or Bronstein, or MOGEN clamps. None of these have received rabbinic approval, and all rabbinic authorities, in Israel and America, have issued halachic rulings forbidding the use of these clamps.

The clamps have become highly popular in the field of surgical circumcision because of their improved hemostasis, or, as surgeons boast, their bloodless surgery. *Truly bloodless surgery would invalidate the ritual act of circumcision.* Even when the clamps allow minimal bleeding, the rabbinic prohibition is nevertheless in effect.

D) Reasons for delaying the bris: medical and halachic.

The bris must be delayed if medical opinion considers the procedure to be threatening to the health of the child because of a physiological abnormality. Such abnormalities include increased bloodclotting time; the existence of an infectious process, even if only in the local area, such as impetigo; or a failure to function properly of one or more of the child's organ systems, such as the cardiac, pulmonary, renal, or hepatic systems. These medical considerations are absolute. The halacha forbids performing the bris until seven days have passed from the time that the doctor considers the baby cured from his affliction. Failure to wait the full seven days poses serious question as to the validity of the bris. In halacha, such a bris is considered as one that was performed before the eighth day.

The halachic standard of pediatric illness is far more demanding than the medical standard. It is quite common for the mohel to express concern for the health of the child, while the pediatrician offers full assurance that the child can safely withstand the minor stresses of the circumcision procedure. The opinion of a well-trained mohel, who has kept up with medical advances, takes precedence over the more lenient opinion of the physician, and the bris must be delayed.

In practice, the incidence of elevated bilirubin causes the most conflict between mohel and physician. It is important to recognize that the understanding of what an elevated bilirubin really means in medical terms is under intense investigation even at this date. There has arisen a word-of-mouth consensus among mohelim who are uncomfortable with new medical information to set a limit on the amount of bilirubin in the blood above which they will not perform the mila. There is no basis for this consensus, not in medicine or in halacha. The issue is not of the numbers, but of the health of the child as determined by deviations from the norm. With the widespread use of computers in hospitals and the availability of statistical records now involving hundreds of thousands of newborns, it has become clear that the norm is indeed a spectrum involving three types of bilirubin, as well as a host of other clinical factors. Therefore, when a dispute arises between a mohel's concern over a slightly elevated bilirubin (or the yellowness of the child, called jaundice), and the advice of the attending pediatrician, who sees no reason to delay the bris, it is essential to consult a rabbi who is well-trained in halacha and medicine, or a yeshiva-trained physician who is fully aware of the importance of the ritual and the overriding concern that halacha has for the health of the child.

The medical issue at hand is really the proper functioning of the liver of the newborn. Every child is born with the liver yet immature. Thus a rise in bilirubin, referred to as "physiological jaundice," is perfectly normal during the first five days of life. The persistence of this condition for an extra day or so is well within the norm, as long as there is evidence that the liver has begun to do its work, as shown by a significant decrease in level of bilirubin. Even if the bilirubin has not dropped below the magical numbers eight or ten or twelve — which the mohelim have selected for some reason — the baby must be classified as healthy in accord with the pediatrician's evaluation. The reluctance of the mohel must then be overcome by rabbinic authority, or another mohel, who is more knowledgeable of the physiological facts concerning jaundice, must be selected.

Occasionally it is possible to determine that a child's jaundice is persisting due to a factor in the milk of his nursing mother. It is improper to suggest that the mother stop nursing even temporarily in order to have the bilirubin drop to a level acceptable to the mohel. The halacha recognizes that nursing is so beneficial to the child that even Sabbath laws may be transgressed to provide mother's milk, even when "formula" is available. The physician's determination that the elevated bilirubin does not in any way endanger the child necessitates that the mila be performed at the proper time, on the eighth day of the child's life.

Evidence that bilirubin may have a beneficial affect on the newborn has just been reported (February 1987)* Bilirubin has been shown to serve as an anti-oxidant and free-radical "scavenger" to protect the sensitive cells of the newborn from metabolic by-products that are injurious.

In cases of anatomical abnormalities, such as severe hypospadia, pediatric surgeons urge that mila be postponed for as long as two years, when the plastic surgery necessary to correct the defect can be performed using the foreskin as the reconstruction material. An Orthodox rabbi well versed in the complexities of the procedure must be consulted for detailed instruction at the time that the surgery is to be performed. A mohel must be present to assist the surgeon in the ritual aspect of the delayed circumcision.

In cases of ambiguous genitalia, often the medical advice is to do reconstructive surgery that will fix the sex of the child as female even though, genetically, as determined by chromosomal analyses and the presence of testes, the child is a male. These cases are most complex, and careful coordination between rabbi and physician is absolutely essential to find a solution that will allow the child to mature in accord with halachic standards and with the greatest measure of personal happiness. Arbitrarily deciding to raise a genetically male child as a female involves many halachic concerns that must be carefully evaluated by the most learned rabbinic authorities.

XIII. THE CARE OF THE INFANT ON SHABBOS AND YOM TOV*

The special problems encountered in infant care on Shabbos and Yom Tov are surmounted with ease if proper preparations are made. The problematic areas most often encountered involve:

A) Body hygiene and diaper disposal
B) Medications
C) Supplementary feedings.

A) Body hygiene.

1. The problem

Sponge, wash cloth, or soap bars cannot be used on Shabbos or Yom Tov.

*See Additional Notes below.

The solution: Absorbent cotton balls, or soft paper tissues prepared to proper size in advance, are used with light petrolatum (mineral) oil for cleansing the diaper area. Since water is not used, many halachic objections are avoided. In addition, the oil does not have the tendency to chill the skin since it does not evaporate at room temperature. This is a special advantage for night time use when the home temperature is reduced.

If it is necessary to use soap and water, a liquid soap can be substituted for the usual bar soap. A wash cloth or sponge that must be "wrung out" is not permitted. A liquid soap solution prepared in a plastic spray bottle can be used to wet the diaper area. Facial tissue, previously cut toilet tissue, or a large absorbent cotton ball can be used to wipe up the excess moisture and to complete the cleaning of the skin folds and crevices.

2. The problem

Diapers must not be "flushed" or rinsed on Shabbos or holidays, nor may they be discarded into a water or detergent-filled pail since this initiates the laundering process, forbidden on these days.

The solution: If it is possible to use throwaway paper diapers, all problems are avoided. The use of adhesive tabs on the disposable diaper as a fastener, or its removal which involves tearing the plastic liner, does not involve any halachic prohibitions. However, this product is not always available nor can all easily assume the expense entailed in their use.

Therefore, the soiled cloth diapers must be placed in a closed container, without any prior treatment, to await laundering after the end of Shabbos or Yom Tov.

B) Medications.

An infant is judged in most situations requiring medication as one who is "ill without danger." Naturally, if there is a serious illness such as fever, serious skin infections, or severe diarrhea, all Sabbath and holiday laws are suspended. For minor problems, medications may be administered if these do not require transgression of Shabbos laws.[19]

1. The problem

Ointments must not be used on Shabbos and Yom Tov.

The solution: If possible, the medication should be made available in powder form or suspended in light oil. If this is not available, the ointment should be applied to a gauze pad before Shabbos. When needed, this pad can be applied to the affected area without any attempt to distribute it over the skin.

Pills or capsules may be crushed on Shabbos for administration to children who cannot swallow the whole capsule or pill.

Vitamins given daily to supplement the diet may be given on Shabbos as well.

Body temperature may be measured on Shabbos if illness is suspected.

In all situations classified as even remotely dangerous to life, all Shabbos and Yom Tov laws are suspended. Any attempts to **avoid** transgression of biblical laws under such circumstances is in itself a serious halachic violation unless this avoidance does not necessitate any loss of time or efficiency in obtaining medical service. If serious illness is suspected, immediate medical attention must be sought even if it is only a little while until the Sabbath ends.

---

19. Adults are forbidden to take any medications on Shabbos for minor aches or pains or for minor dermatological conditions. The use of a protective cover over a wound (Example: Band-Aid) is not classified as a medication and is permissable. Nor is the use of liquid sun tan preparation classified as a medication.

C) Supplementary feeding.

1. The problem

It is forbidden to open cans on Shabbos, or to warm cold liquids by placing them on the stove.

The solution: (a) The usual procedure is to prepare the required number of nursing bottles before Shabbos and to refrigerate them until needed. A large supply of hot water must be kept on the fire to warm the cold nursing bottle. This warming can be done only by withdrawing some hot water into an appropriate-sized vessel and then placing the bottle in this vessel when it is **not on the stove or blech.***

(b) A simplified procedure is to prepare the baby formula double-strength by omitting half the required amount of water while maintaining the quantity of solids. When needed, the bottle can be reconstituted by withdrawing the required amount of hot water into a small cup and adding it to the bottle, thus diluting and warming the bottle simul-taneously. If whole milk is used, a can of evaporated milk, which is double-strength whole milk, can be used. With the pediatrician's approval, the bottles need not be prepared in advance. For example, if an 8-ounce bottle of milk is needed, 4 ounces of evaporated milk is poured from a previously punctured and refrigerated can into a clean bottle. Four ounces of hot water are then withdrawn into a small cup or another clean bottle and added to the milk. This results in 8 ounces of warmed, reconstituted milk with the use of only 4 ounces of hot water.

This procedure can be used even if the infant is on a special formula. The formula is made up double-strength and ster-ilized in bulk in a suitably large container. When needed, equal quantities of refrigerated formula and hot water are added to a clean nursing bottle and fed to the infant. Since the nursing bottle is not used to store the milk for extended time periods, most doctors do not require that these bottles be

*See Additional Notes below.

sterile — only washed clean with soap or detergent.

(c) A **dry** glass bottle or nipple may be sterilized on Shabbos by immersing them in the kettle of hot water kept on the Shabbos blech.*

Grinding or chopping food.

In preparing fruit or meat for babies, a mill or grinder cannot be used on Shabbos and Yom Tov. Bananas can be mashed with a fork just prior to serving. Meat which must be prepared in a food mill or grinder should be prepared before Shabbos and Yom Tov. To avoid spoilage, this preparation must be made from freshly cooked meat which should be ground while still hot, subdivided into portion units and quickly refrigerated or frozen until used.

Instant puddings.

The preparation of instant puddings which involves the jelling or "setting" the milk into a custard-like consistency is not permitted on Shabbos but may be done on Yom Tov.

The use of an enzyme preparation to curdle milk as in the cheese-making process is forbidden on Shabbos and Yom Tov.

Additional notes on the care of the infant on Shabbos and Yom Tov.

A. Toys: The wind-up swing.

If the swing can function manually and is not rigidly locked into place unless it is activated, then it is permissible to wind up the spring so that it will sway automatically.

B. Aerosol sprays.

If the product undergoes an irreversible change of physical state, it must not be used on Shabbos or Yom Tov. The use

*See Additional Notes below.

of an aerosol antiseptic or dermatological preparation such as steroid foams for a child with eczema is permitted. However, the use of an aerosol packed parve whipped cream which is fluffed and fixed into a different state during the removal process is to be avoided.

The electric stove.

The electric stove presents a special problem for Yom Tov use. Most commercial stoves function with a bimetallic thermostat. This means that changing the setting involves making and breaking the electric current — a forbidden act on Yom Tov.

Suggested solution.

If not standard equipment, an electrician can construct a panel board to which each burner will be connected. When the burner circuit is activated, a neon light will glow as long as the current is flowing. Thus it will be possible to ascertain if the bimetallic thermostat is in the "make" (on) phase or the "break" (off) phase. When the light is on, the cooking temperature may be raised. When the light is off the dial may be moved to a lower or an "off" setting if no other cooking is being contemplated. Of course, once the burner is turned to the "off" setting, it cannot be reset on Yom Tov.

Pesach Medications

Most tablet or capsule pharmaceuticals do not present any special problems for Pesach use. The active ingredients are never classified as *chometz* and the inert diluents usually present no problem more severe than that due to use of corn starch as a binder. Since corn is not one of the "five grains" but is classified as a "bean product" *(kitniyos)* it can be approved for medicinal use as an inert ingredient in a tablet or capsule.

Liquid medications do pose a special problem. These preparations or elixirs used especially in the treatment of asthmatic or allergic conditions may contain up to 10% grain alcohol — a forbidden ingredient on Pesach. The physician should be asked to prescribe tablets or capsules rather than such elixirs. If the liquid form is absolutely necessary to permit more efficient administration under emergency conditions or for pediatric use, these tablets can be crushed and dissolved in wine or kosher syrup water of known quantity, e.g., 6 teaspoons measure approximately one ounce. Dissolve 6 tablets in one ounce of wine to give a "6 dose" bottle for emergency use.

If time permits, it is advisable to have the pharmacist make up the preparation from pure active ingredients using wine or Pesach brandy which you provide.

If it is necessary to use an existing elixir it should be diluted before Pesach so that its alcohol content (5% in NOVAHISTINE DH) can be diluted with twice the volume of wine or syrup water. If the suggested dose was one teaspoon (5 ml.), a tablespoon (15 ml.) dose should now be used. The purpose of this dilution is to reduce the alcohol content to approximately 1.6% or less than 1:60.

PART II

Purity of Heart and Mind

XIV. POPULATION CONTROL — THE JEWISH VIEW

The world's increasing population is viewed by many as one of the basic problems of our time. The "demographic problem" or, as referred to in the lay press, the "population explosion," has received the attention of the best minds of the fields of medicine, economics, law, and religion. Reports of authoritative decisions reflecting the Catholic, Protestant and Jewish viewpoints appear with annoying repetition. This paper is offered firstly to summarize and clarify the Torah view of the demographic problem, and secondly as a cry of protest against those who took unto themselves the mantle of spokesman for the Jewish people on this complex and delicate issue.

The penalty for the failure of the Orthodox community to speak out on the great issues of the day is twofold. The truths of our Torah are unavailable as guidelines for our people, and many who should be silent represent themselves as prophets of Judaism. The validation of a prophecy occurs when there is absolute concurrence between the prophetic message and the prophecy of Moses — our Torah teachings. Based on this criterion, we must conclude that the topic of population control has attracted a disproportionate number of false prophets whose teachings weaken rather than strengthen the hearts of our people.

For almost a decade, I have had the unique opportunity of conducting a seminar series in *Hilkhot Nida* for the senior students at Yeshiva University. The laws relevant to the principle and practices of birth-control techniques comprise a significant part of these seminars. Despite the lucidity and accuracy that is the teacher's reward from the student-teacher counter-current,[1] I approach my task with trepidation. What right do I have to don the mantle of spokesman? Indeed I claim none. Let

---

1. *Ta'anit* 7a.

no one read into my words the language of *Pesak Din* — a language reserved for the ears or eyes of the individual questioner on this complex, intimately personal problem. I present for considered judgment a point of view based on the primary sources of our faith — the words of the Talmud and its commentaries. It is my hope that it will serve to counter-balance the views already expressed by others.

Definition of the problem: Recent advances in disease control have given new impetus to the recurring Malthusian nightmare of world population outstripping world food supply. Unless vigorous action is taken to correct the imbalance of a declining death rate coupled to a burgeoning birth rate, mankind is irrevocably committed to a catastrophic famine.

The Torah attitude consists of the composite answer to the following questions:

A) Are the facts presented accurate?

In the many publications presented to the lay public, the basic mathematics of the Malthusian nightmare goes unchallenged. Historically speaking, the projections of Malthus were totally inaccurate. He failed to allow for the scientific and technological advances that have kept food production increases ahead of population growth. Indeed, at the World Conference on Populations, organized under the auspices of the United Nations in September 1965, many expressed the opinion that[2] "there was no problem of excessive rates of growth in underdeveloped areas and thereby no public or private action was needed." This was confirmed by many studies published in 1987.[3]

B) What are the philosophical or ethical implications of projected programs to reduce the birth rate?

The conflict of science and religion was once limited to the

2. *Science,* vol. 151, Jan. 14, 1966.
3. *Science,* vol. 236, no. 4797, April 3, 1987; *Science Times,* Sept. 9, 1987.

question of the authenticity of the Torah. In the 19th century the challenge to the Torah came from the evolutionists. In our time the spotlight is focused on the methodology of natural science. The challenge to Torah values stems from the claim that the methods of natural science constitute man's only reliable access to the knowledge of reality.

Those familiar with the personal letters of Charles Darwin know that he first lost faith in God as a Judge and Ruler and then rejected Him as a Creator. Evident from the writings of many of the leaders in the study of the demographic problem is the conviction that the Darwinian refutation of God, the Creator, compels us to discount Him as an active force in the affairs of mankind. In the halakhic sense, if the God of Shabbos does not exist then the God of the Exodus is equally nonexistent.

Such is not the Torah view! The management of the world's population is relegated unto God.[4] The insistence that God erred in not realizing the mathematical certainty of a geo-metrically increasing population outstripping arithmetical in-creases in food supply is but another manifestation of the theology of blasphemy which is in vogue today. Inherent in our concept of a personal God is the philosophy of the verse in Psalm 145 in which God is praised for providing sustenance for all His creatures. Food supply and world population are areas of divine concern.

However, man has been granted a junior partnership in the management of this world. Imbued with the spark of Divine intelligence, man is permitted, even required, to use his part-nership rights to regulate his own affairs, on condition that he does not violate the by-laws of this God-man relationship that are formulated in the Torah. What if the present projections prove to be more accurate than those made by Malthus? We are told that at the present rate of increase in world population, 300 million tons of *additional* grain annually will be needed by 1980. This is more grain than is now produced by all of North America! What guidelines have been set down for our instruc-tion in this yet hypothetical situation?

4. *Rosh Hashanah* 1:5; *Yevamot* 62b-63; cf. Rashi *ad locum.*

The Jew as a world citizen is personally concerned with famine in India and China.[5] However the Noahidic laws which serve as Torah (instruction) for all humanity demand a proper sequence of actions. Before a Jew can support birth-control clinics in overpopulated areas of the world, he must insist that there be heroic efforts made to utilize fully the agricultural potential of the world. This implies the extension of modern farming technology to all parts of the world, as well as a more effective and more morally responsible distribution of food surpluses. It is ludicrous to maintain that an Indian will allow himself to be surgically sterilized, his wife aborted or implanted with a plastic loop, bow, or spiral, yet he will obstinately refuse to use a better grain seed, add chemical fertilizers to his land, or adjust his plowing pattern so as to minimize water loss.

It is equally untenable to insist that the logistics of world-wide food distribution present insurmountable obstacles. A nation that can transport the men and material needed to wage modern war in Korea and Vietnam can, with efficiency and dispatch, overcome all obstacles in the way of food distribution. Surely we have adequate motivation. Is it more immoral to allow a family to lose its political freedom than to sit idly by while it loses its personal freedom to bear children? At a prophetic symposium,[6] a leading professor of political science bravely presented a prognosis that clearly spells the doom of the concept of the integrity and worth of the individual upon which all democratic principles depend. He predicted, "Inescapably there will be changes in our most intimate habits and patterns of living. It is not enough to have a pill. People must be willing to take it — in many cases not merely to prevent the birth of unwanted children, but even to prevent the birth of deeply wanted, even longed-for children. The time may not be far off when some societies, at least, may find themselves pressed by unyielding circumstances into an extraordinary invasion of

5. *Ta'anit* 11a. Cf. *Derishah* on *Orach Chayim* 574:5.
6. "Time for Decision: The Biological Crossroads," University of Colorado School of Medicine, June 1966.

human privacy — the limitation of births by legal ordinance, with severe penalties for infraction." The threat of communism pales in comparison with this summary of the nightmare of "1984" materializing because man lacks the humility to admit that there are areas that are immune to his encroachments. China has indeed legislated against the "longed for and wanted" child by limiting all families to one child together with severe penalties for each additional child. The nightmare of yesteryear is the reality of 1987. Can any moral individual concern himself with abortion clinics before he has suggested, nay demanded, that our resources be committed to increase meat and poultry production, tap the wealth of the oceans, and then develop new sources of high quality proteins from the algal and microbial cultures studied experimentally these last few years? The idea that an illiterate African, Asian, or South American would rather starve than accept a diet "strange" to him, has been fully disproved by the Incaparina Program in South America. Under this program, teams of nutritionists educated the protein-starved masses to accept a flour composed of corn, sesame or soy oil, yeast, and vitamin A. New recipes were accepted by the "illiterate masses" with the resultant upgrading of the national diet of millions of people. There must be unanimity in the conviction that we dare not dump potatoes, burn excess wheat, cut back on production quotas, and then make impassioned pleas for free distribution of contraceptive devices as a humanitarian effort to prevent world-wide famine.

Let us assume, once again, the hypothetical situation of worldwide food shortages uncompensated by our best utilization of the latest technological advances in food production. The question to be answered is:

C) Are there religiously acceptable means of artificially limiting family size?

All people, Jew and non-Jew, are enjoined to procreate. The philosophy of the halakhah is clearly opposed to any limitation of family size.[7] Abstinence is hardly more in compliance with the spirit of the halachah than are other more artificial means of contraception. Only when proper motivation for family planning can be ascertained does specific methodology become the critical issue. Any halachic principle that requires the prior determination of unexpressed motivations proves to be most difficult to legislate. Thought processes are so variable among different people, that whenever possible overt acts are substituted by our Sages for the equally authoritative intellectual commitments.[7]

Poverty that threatens a family's physical and spiritual welfare may indeed be adequate motivation for the use of acceptable contraceptive methods or for delaying marriage until there is an improvement in the financial situation.[8] However, poverty has many interpretations. The psychological poverty of the $50,000 income family surrounded by families with $90,000 yearly incomes must be clearly differentiated from the physiological poverty of the protein-starved Peruvian or Indian. The demarcation line between necessity and luxury has been obliterated so often during the maturation of the economies of the western nations, that objective criteria for a universal standard of living must be established before the need for population control can be evaluated.[9]

Many of the population-control techniques being proposed for mass use are categorically unacceptable to Judaism. Surgical intervention, in the form of vasectomies (male), oophorectomies and tubal litigations (female), or abortions, is forbidden

7. Cf. *Yevamot* 39b.

8. *Shulchan Aruch, Even Haezer* 1, 3 and 8; Maimonides, *Hilchot Deot* 5:11.

9. *Ta'anit* 11; *Orach Chayim* 574:5.
This reference has little relevance despite its erroneous application to our discussion by previous authors. Firstly the prohibition is one of abstaining from pleasurable activity when the populace is in distress and applies with equal force to calamitous childhood epidemics or wide-spread infertility. Secondly, the exemption of the *tevilah* night from this prohibition minimizes its impact on the birth rate since this is usually the period of peak fertility for the wife.

to both Jew and non-Jew unless necessitated by life-threatening medical emergencies. Abortion is included in the Noahidic prohibition of murder. Surgical induction of male infertility (*sirus*) may likewise be proscribed in the universally applicable Noahide laws. The use of the intrauterine contraceptive devices (I.U.C.D.) such as the Grafenberg rings of the 1920's or their modern counterparts designed by Margulies and others, present unique problems to halakhic authorities. Medical scientists have yet to fully elucidate the mechanism of contraceptive action of the I.U.C.D. If the evidence we now have proves accurate, contraception is accomplished by increasing uterine or tubal contractions. The resulting expulsion of the fertilized ovum is actually an early abortion. Abortions prior to 40 days of conception are halakhically differentiated from true abortion that is equated with murder. However it is clearly prohibited unless there be adequate justification based on medical or other equally valid grounds. The recently proposed post-coital contraceptive pills must be equated with the I.U.C.D. since their effectiveness is the result of abortificant action.[10]

If all ancillary criteria for their use are met, the anovulatory pills, or the use of a mechanical barrier with or without chemical spermicides (condom and diaphragm method) may be acceptable for use by the non-Jewish populace that is obligated to the observance of the Noahide laws. Three experimental techniques, unavailable as yet for mass use, may also prove to be acceptable. I refer to the use of various drugs by the husband to inhibit sperm formation; the injection of a silicone plug into the sperm duct to prevent the passage of sperm, but with the important feature of easy removal to restore fertility; and the infertility that can be induced by immunological means.

There are different guidelines for the Jew on this question of population control. If reduction in the birth rate of the famine-threatened population of the world is indeed the proper response, then the Jew as a world citizen should join in the worldwide effort of providing contraceptive materials to those desir-

10. Recent findings raise the question of a possible abortificant action by the anovulatory pills.

ous of limiting family size. The Jew as a Jew must at this time reject the suggestion that he, too, limit the size of his family. We have unique problems created for us by world citizenry. Six and one half million Jews destroyed at the hands of world citizenry in one generation represents a staggering loss. When calculated on the Malthusian geometric tables it represents an astronomical loss of our life blood. Only a total lack of moral and historic responsibility can explain the present-day statistics which show our brethen leading the list of ethnic groups with the lowest birth rates in America. Their motivation is that of an egotistic hedonist, rather than of a world citizen sleepless from nights of Malthusian nightmares. Reduction of family size must be justified only on a personal, familial basis, not as part of the demographic problem.

For the observant Jew, the use of any contraceptive device introduces new halakhic considerations. The basic prohibitions are well known. Onanism, and the *condom method* which is tantamount to onanism, is clearly a biblical prohibition. Many halakhic authorities classify the *diaphragm method* as "casting the seed on wood and stones" and prohibit its use even if life-threatening medical consideration demands contraception.[11] The use of non-mechanical barriers to conception such as chemical spermicidals or hormonal repression of ovulation present us with the least objectionable methodology for contraception. However the hormonal contraceptives pose a new problem.[12] Many women find that the "pill" induces intermenstrual bleeding. The earlier dosage forms caused such major or minor spotting in 65% of the women, especially during the first 3 months of use. Such spotting induces the state of *nidah* (menstrual bleeding) which necessitates abstinence and *mikvah* with all the *Halakhot* of menstrual bleeding. The use of I.U.C.D. likewise is often accompanied by intermenstrual spotting. If this spotting be due to physiological modification rather than mechanical damage to the uterine wall, then this too is true *nidah*. The newer low-dosage "pills", and new designs of the I.U.C.D., may minimize the problem of *nidah*. However, no

11. Rabbi Akiba Eiger, *Responsa*, 71.

observant Jew can consider their use except under the constant supervision of a competent halakhic authority.

The use of hormonal or chemical inhibitors of spermatogenesis, or of the temporary interference with sperm passage, is prohibited to the Jew. The use of chemical spermicides or the yet experimental induction of immunological infertility, or the use of injected high dosage progesterones which appear to inhibit ovulation without the problem of intermenstrual spotting, offer the best possibilities for halakhically acceptable contraception for the family that must use artificial contraceptive techniques.

The concept of proper motivation as a prerequisite for any halakhic evaluation of the contraceptive technique to be used, requires further elaboration. *Emunah* (Faith) and *Bitachon* (Trust) are not psychological crutches. They are the natural laws of our existence. The big sacrifice, the *Akedat Yitzchak* (the sacrifice of Isaac) is rarely demanded of us. However the small daily acts of sacrifice that are the basis of our survival as a Holy Nation, should be woven into the personality fabric of every Jew. It may be "inconvenient" to measure every thought and act against the yardstick of Torah right and wrong. Indeed to live the life of a human being clearly differentiated by his every act from those infrahuman species that are his co-tenants on this planet, is a major inconvenience. The Torah concerns itself with every aspect of our personal and interpersonal life.[12] When probing one's own motivation for family planning there must be a differentiation between proper motives and those that reflect the flaws in the Torah personality. When a Yeshiva trained young man presents to the halakhic authority motives such as: We want time to get to know each other better; we

12. The health safety aspect of contraceptive pills or mechanical devices is also of Halakhic concern. Man is required by Torah Law to avoid all acts that may prove injurious. In May 1966, the "pills" were reported on by a 12-member Scientific group of the World Health Organization. In general they found risks to be "minimal" with the warning that doctors keep alert to individual idiosyncracies, and that the possibility of long-term harmful effects cannot be excluded.

would like to travel first; if my wife can work we can raise our standard of living, he simultaneously reveals that the years of Torah training had little impact on his personality. Even if the absence of a second income necessitates continued parental support, there is little validity to the claim of financial hardship. It is a misdirected sense of dignity that dictates that money may be borrowed from parents for the purchase of a car, a home, even for travel tickets, but not to permit fuller compliance with our Torah regulations.

Competent halakhic authority may under specific circumstances permit the use of some contraceptive techniques. Any permission granted is based on major and minor details of the particular situation. Such permission is "non-transferable" and "non-extendable" in time. It is a *Pesak Halakhah* in its finest, purest, and most legalistic form. In general the following factors would first be carefully evaluated:

(a) What are the true motivations of husband and wife that induced them to seek halakhic permission?

(b) Has there been minimum compliance with the commandment, "to be fruitful"?

(c) What specific contraceptive technique is being considered?

(d) What is the medical status of husband and wife? Psychological as well as physiological factors are most significant.

(e) What is the financial status of the family?

The Torah attitude toward family planning is the consequence of its teachings about the function and purpose of the marital act. A full treatment of these teachings is beyond the scope of this paper. We are taught that the purpose of the sexual union is far more encompassing than merely the biological generative function. The laws of *nidah*, the commandment "to be fruitful," the details of *mitzvat ona* that recognizes the sexual rights of the wife, the laws of *Mikvah* and the laws that determine our position on contraception, all join to formulate a philosophy of family life for the Jew. It is a program of refinement in thought and act so that the individual can fulfill his duties and obligations inherent in this intimate association of a man, his wife, his people and his God.

XV. EMBRYO TRANSFER AND GONAD TRANSPLANT: HALACHIC PERSPECTIVES

Introduction:

Therapy for infertility involves a sensitive balance for weighing the relative importance of rights, duties, and privileges in conflict. These include the right of a husband and wife to procreate; the rights of a fetus or preembryo to life; the interest of society in preserving its ethical foundations; and the hard reality that scarce resources must be allocated amongst many worthy projects, thus pitting many goods against each other. It is indeed ironic, in light of the Judaeo-biblical heritage that provides the ethical foundation for much of Western civilization, that the right *not* to procreate is more clearly accepted within the legal framework of America's society than the right to procreate, using non–coital techniques. This is especially true for protocols requiring the assistance of a third party donor. The ethical analyses of embryo transfer (ET) and gonadal transplantation (GT) here presented applies with but minor differences to other protocols of non–coital reproduction such as AIH and AID.

A) The natural and the nature of man

The allure of the natural has never been stronger. The artificial is equated with the abnormal and even the immoral. Therefore many sterility management techniques that apply the magnificent advances in reproductive biology of this decade have been declared illicit by the Catholic Church. (Doctrinal statement: Instruction on respect for human life in its origin and on the dignity of procreation, May 10, 1986.) Even when the more obvious moral concerns, such as preembryo wastage, masturbation or third party intrusion into the conjugal relationship, do not apply, the separation of the sex act from the procreation process is considered illicit because it "deprives human procreation of the dignity which is proper and co-natural to it."

The Judaeo-biblical tradition does not concur with this concern for the "co-natural." The natural does not represent a moral category but is merely an ecological niche or a social state early in the development of human society. In Genesis 1:28 we learn that God blessed them and said to them: "Be fruitful and multiply, fill the earth and *master it*." There is a dual command in this verse. The first is to have children, to procreate. The second is to become an active participant in the process of molding the world to suit the needs of humankind. This active interventionist role encompasses the pursuit of all knowledge for the betterment of mankind. We are obligated, by divine decree, to lift the veils off the hidden face of nature. The "non-natural" thus represents no more than man's fulfillment of this divine command.

B) The duty to heal

To heal the sick is a biblical imperative (Exodus 21:19; Deuteronomy 22:2; Leviticus 19:17). Infertility is viewed as an illness akin to other non-physiological conditions. Biblical language underscores the severity of this illness. When Rachel appeals to Jacob for help (Genesis 30:18) she cries out "Give me children or else I die." The cure of so significant an illness justifies the assumption of some modicum of risk to the patient, as well as the sensitive concern of those who can offer help. This risk, however, is often shared by the fetus and thus the concern of the health professional must often encompass whole family and social groupings.

C) The ethical import of embryo transfer (ET)

The transfer of an autologous embryo, as in the IVF technique using sperm from the husband, an egg from the wife, does not raise any serious ethical issues. Indeed, until the recent blanket disapproval of almost all techniques used in infertility management by the Vatican, it was assumed that a consensus existed among ethicists of all faiths to approve autologous embryo transplants. From the Judaeo-biblical heritage, these techniques conform with the Divine instruction to master the physical and biological world by lifting another veil from the face of nature. The oligospermic husband, the wife with blocked Fallopian tubes, can now be given the opportunity of having children whose cells contain their own hereditary material.

The ethical issues raised by this protocol apply to many other procedures used in infertility management. They are:

a) risk to mother
b) risk to fetus
c) semen procurement: special concern for Jewish Orthodox patients
d) egg retrieval and disposal — preembryo wastage

a) *risk to mother*

The protocol requires exogenous hormonal treatment. Oocytes are recovered by laproscopy or by an ultrasound-directed needle transvaginally. This is an invasive protocol incurring a low level risk to the wife both from the hormonal manipulation and the surgical harvest of oocytes. It is the consensus of most physicians and ethicists that the risk/benefit ratio is clearly in favor of doing the procedure.

b) *risk to fetus*

All evidence to date has failed to reveal any special danger of fetal malformation due to the mechanical manipulation of the egg; its exposure to the exogenous hormones taken by the wife; or to the culturing fluid used during the initial cell divisions in the petri plate. Even if there were a significant risk of malformation, the protocol would still be acceptable since the alternative is not to be born to the most severe "malformation" possible! Surely, if alternate protocols develop, with quantitatively different risk rates, the protocol of lowest risk must be selected.

c) *semen procurement:* a special concern for Jews observant of ritual law.

Biblical law prohibits masturbation. The "wasting of seed" is the moral concern but within the ritual code of Judaism manual

masturbation is particularly prescribed. It is therefore necessary to obtain sperm during the normal marital act by means of a
special condom such as a milex sheath or other material non-
injurious to sperm.

If the wife has a short menstrual cycle, the marital laws of
Judaism requiring abstinence during the first twelve or more
days of the cycle may present a special problem if ovulation
occurs before this time. Storing semen from the previous
month's cycle is the preferred solution to this problem. If this be
not feasible, a recognized rabbinic authority must be consulted
to discuss alternate means of semen procurement.

d) *pre-embryo wastage*

An excess embryo, if not implanted, may be frozen and saved
for a second attempt if pregnancy does not occur at first try.
Hormonal priming of the wife must be repeated to prepare the
uterus for implantation. These preembryos have no ethical or
moral import prior to implantation since there is no possibility
of their further development. It would be better to dispose of
them rather than to salvage them by donation to those who are
infertile because of ovarian failure. Our concern for consanguinity and the impact of E.T. on the sanctity, cohesiveness,
and sense of mutual dependence of the family is the basis for
this recommendation.

D) Donor sperm: adultery, bastardy, and consanguinity

The Judaeo-biblical tradition differentiates between "un-
sanctified" sexual relations and adulterous relationships. Adulterous relationships, which impose the stigma of bastardy on
the offspring of these unions, are those involving incest or
"betrayal" by a married woman. Infidelity, an act of "betrayal"
of the husband's trust does not occur under the medical protocol of embryo transfer using donor sperm for fertilization.
There is no adultery with a hypodermic syringe! Thus the key
concerns are for the psychological impact on the infertile
couple, and for the "domino effect," lest this procedure be not
limited to cases in which the family unit is to be preserved and

strengthened. Unmarried women, lesbians, those seeking sperm of "superior" males to endow their children with special genetic traits, should not avail themselves of the procedures of AID or ET.

Scrupulous attention must be paid to the medical and genetic background of the donor. The effort in doing so is significant. There is therefore a tendency to use a screened donor repetitively. This increases the possibility of consanguineous marriages of such offspring, with the resulting religious and genetic concerns. There must be a limit placed on the number of inseminations permitted one donor, and concentration of patients from a small sub-set of society who because of religious or nationalistic associations gravitate to one or two gynecologists, must be avoided.

E) Cryopreservation of sperm, eggs, and preembryos

The key ethical concern involves the danger of injury and malformations due to the freezing-thawing protocol. Additional research, and experimental clinical application when the risk/benefit ratio is favorable, will clarify the validity of this concern.

Paternity and maternity

The sperm with its genetic material determines the paternity of the fetus. The "artificiality" of AID or ET does not alter this conclusion, clearly held by all biblical authorities. The issue of maternity is more complex. For the first time in human history, gestational motherhood can be separated from genetic motherhood. Surely the contributions of the gestational mother are quite consequential. Legal (halachic) authorities in Judaism have not been able to clarify this dilemma, and therefore consanguinity prohibitions must be applied to "both" mother's families.

Gonadal transplant

Although the clinical application of this technique lies in the future, the analysis of its ethical import is a proper concern for the present. Too often, medical technology outspaces ethical and moral analyses.

Two types of issues are involved: one biological and genetic; the other, religious concern for consanguinity.

Obviously, the genetics of gametes produced from a transplanted gonad will be that of the donor. Thus, biological inbreeding will result, if children produced by the recipient of the transplant should marry into the family of the donor. This must be avoided by proper record keeping, which always poses a risk to the privacy of all concerned. Surely some innovative procedure can be designed to address both concerns.

The issue of consanguinity is blurred by the transplant of gonads rather than gametes. As previously discussed, sperm impose paternity. Ova carry maternity of the donor, which must be shared with the gestational maternity of the recipient. When gonads are transplanted, only the genetic potential of the donor is transferred. No gametes result, until the gonad is "gestated" by the recipient. There is adequate biblical precedent to assume that this grafting procedure results in a loss of the original genetic identity of the gonad. All subsequent gametes produced are therefore fully identified with the recipient in so far as religious law is concerned.

Throughout human history there has been a tension between the "trees of the garden from which you may eat" and the "tree of knowledge" forbidden to man. Intellectual integrity, sensitivity to personal and social ethics, and to the educative role of society, are the guarantors that this tension will result in progress for the betterment of mankind.

XVI. ETHICAL IMPLICATIONS OF THE DRUG CULTURE

Last year approximately 250 million prescriptions for mood-modifying drugs were filled by the pharmacists of our nation.

This chapter appeared in *Judaism and Drugs*, 1973, *Federation of Jewish Philanthropies of New York.*

Estimates are that one-third of the adult population had such prescriptions written for them. To this staggering total must be added the widespread use of non-prescription drugs for the treatment of nervous tension, tension headaches, nervous stomach, etc.

The pharmaceutical industry with the cooperation of the medical profession have redefined, as problems requiring medical treatment, a wide range of human behavior patterns that were previously considered to be variants of normal behavioral responses to environmental stimuli. Powerful psychoactive drugs are recommended for college freshmen to mitigate the anxieties that confront them in their new environment; for newlyweds to assist them in their interpersonal adjustments; for the newly bereaved to blunt the impact of their tragic loss; or for children moving to a new neighborhood where social adjustments will impose new tensions and new anxieties.

This widespread use of drugs for the treatment of non-pathological conditions is an American phenomenon. Modern man, cut loose from his ancient moorings in the Judaeo-biblical traditions, has turned to the pharmacopeia as his surrogate bible, and meticulously heeds the categorical imperatives of nerve cell physiology and biochemistry in a saddening parody of Kantian ethics. It is particularly disturbing to postulate that this socially sanctioned trust and faith in chemical solutions to the problems of social and personal maturation, may facilitate the initial experimentation with illegal drugs. Years of training have instilled the Pavlovian reflex of turning toward the medicine chest at the first sign of stress or psychological discomfort. This training is further reinforced by a sophisticated sales campaign that introduces elements of peer acceptability or status, even for the use of illegal drugs. The drug culture we now see about us is but the expected consequence of this training.

Admittedly there is a deep chasm that separates the tranquilized, energized, and neutralized hypochondriac, from the "acid-head" or heroin addict who is devastated in body and soul. But there is a narrow foot-bridge that spans this gap that the adventuresome of spirit or the aimlessly wandering school drop-out may cross. This bridge associates the respected society member with his anarchistic, asocial, anti-establishment opponents. It consists of a shared opinion as to the nature of man. What is this creature man? Who is he? Is he indeed the apex of creation, "clothed in dignity and glory," of infinite worth and inestimable value, as taught by the finely honed ethical system that directed Jewish societies for 3300 years? Or is man the evolutionary resultant of random mutations, whose sense of destiny is but the urgings of his own ego? Is he not an animal among animals, nature bound to pursue an existence of hedonistic egotism? If this latter definition be accurate, then indeed man should be free to "blow his mind, drop-out, cop-out, and trip out" if these activities gratify his needs of the moment. Let others, whose concepts of self-interest be different, choose the awesome responsibility of carrying the world on their shoulders in order to gain an ecological niche in a biotic world!

How does Torah ethics view this drug scene? This view is expressed in the language of *halakhah*. To the Jew firmly rooted in the historical traditions of his people, the *halakhah* is the final development of God's natural law for human societies. It guides and instructs, in legalistic terms, but from the vantage point of three millennia of experimentation in the behavioral sciences. The *halakhah* speaks to man's unique personality, is sensitive to his animalistic needs and his human yearnings. It is therefore universal ethics, equally valid and authoritative despite the varied and alien value systems, that compete for the Jew's allegiance.

Halakhic analysis reveals four distinct areas of concern:
I)   motivation and goal-seeking
II) medical-moral evaluation of the use of noxious substances
III) the discipline of law
IV) the moral consequences of group associations and identification

A) The problem of motivation and goal seeking.

Why resort to psychoactive drugs? The most widespread

motivation is the desire to escape unpleasant realities. Is this desire morally justifiable? In the Torah ethical system freedom from stress is not an absolute good. Freedom from anxiety, fear, or subjugation to higher authority is often equated with moral decadence or the descent of man into the muck and mire of his animal passions. Man is differentiated from infra-human species because he was granted a "Godly image" when he was implanted with the spark of Divine intelligence evidenced in our ability to reason. This great gift was accompanied by freedom to choose — free will. Man is truly free when he has the ability and opportunity to accept and fulfill the responsibilities that accompany his role as the only creature endowed with true intelligence. Any internal or external circumstance that inhibits this free choice is a delimiting of his freedom and an interference with his human role in world society.

This freedom must be defended. There are overt attacks, easily perceived. Inquisitions, antisemitic laws, and quota systems, to mention but a few, are well known enemies. But attacks from within against our human freedoms are more serious. Man can be bound in chains of non-human habituations without his becoming aware of the encirclement, until it is too late. The human ethical organism has an early warning system to signal the approach of the enemy. Anxiety, guilt-feelings, and a sense of shame are the defense mechanisms protecting man's ethical being. When afflicted with the soul-threatening affliction of unbridled ego, insensitivity to the inestimable worth of a friend or neighbor, or even to the preservation of his own family unit, these defense mechanisms energize man into initiating corrective behavior. It is an act of ethical suicide to short-circuit these warning systems by swallowing a capsule, smoking a cigarette, or spraying on a mist of alcoholic extinguishers of the soul fire. Reactive man, discontented man, searching man, becomes under drug influence for varying lengths of time, a lobotomized caricature of this noble creature that bears the Godly image.

When drugs are used persistently rather than occasionally, a new factor is introduced. The Jew is committed to a patterned life style. His day is punctuated by numerous statutory duties and obligations. The need to sleep, exigencies of illness or accident may interfere with these obligations and disrupt the pattern of Jewish living. Free man dare not relinquish his rights and duties voluntarily. To do so is to choose enslavement over freedom. When the momentary enjoyment of drug mediated euphoria is fixed as a component of the daily life pattern, we have man in defeat, with the enemy so omnipresent as to preclude any future hope of turning defeat into victory. The injection of an addictive or mind-destroying drug is an act of physical mutilation of those neural pathways that in composite are the physiological basis of human behavior. The motivation for this self mutilation is the refusal to accept the burden of the "Yoke of Mitzvos."

Some of the theologians of the drug cult have claimed a constructive intent in the use of some of the powerful psychoactive agents. They claim to be in search of a new awareness of Self and God. They seek a heightened receptivity to the myriad of stimuli impinging on their consciousness. They even claim new religious experiences under drug influence. These claims are indeed a psychological phenomenon, one of *déja vue*. We lived through historical periods in which such claims led to great destruction within the Jewish nation. To the Bible scholar it brings to mind the "strange fire" that preoccupied the great and noble sons of Aaron and led to their destruction. To the historian it brings to mind the hallucinatory piety of the false messiah Shabbetai Zevi, whose degradation of body and soul was rationalized as an attempt to experience the "sparks of sanctity," and to liberate the imprisoned soul that inhabits our body and also serves as the energizer of the universe around us. The new religious experiences proved to be but symptoms of mental aberration and spiritual degradation. If there be "new" religious experiences for man to undertake, he can not justify the expenditures of time and energy in metaphysical space probes until he has more successfully investigated his own nature and gained more complete mastery over the earth-bound backyard of his soul.

B) Drugs as noxious substances.

Man is not the master of his body. He is the guardian of both body and soul. As such he is charged with the awesome responsibility to protect both from the many antagonistic influences in his environment. Suicide is no less murder because it is a "victimless" crime. Man is forbidden to victimize himself.

Biblical law forbids man to endanger his life or to cause self-injury unless it is to preserve life or avoid more serious injury. The physical effects of addictive or psychoactive drugs have therefore an ethical component. Good health practices and hygienic standards are ethical imperatives. The incontrovertible fact that the use of LSD or hard drugs, the over-indulgence in alcoholic beverages to the point of acute or chronic alcoholism, or the excessive inhalation of tobacco smoke does damage one or more organ systems, makes these conducts ethically and morally abhorrent.

Our halakhah formally recognizes the omnipresence of noxious substances or potentially dangerous situations (viz. Shabbat 129b). Bridge construction, coal and silver mining, or working with high speed machinery is fraught with danger. Surely there is less potential risk in sitting at home than in crossing a busy thoroughfare. Yet crossing the street is not considered to be an ethical issue demanding prior soul-searching evaluation. The Torah system differentiates various human activities on the basis of social acceptability, economic need, and degree of productivity. Drug usage may be no more dangerous than "dare-devil" activities. But it is motivated by anti-social, non-productive or nihilistic tendencies in man. As such it is morally unjustifiable and ethically prohibited.

C) The moral issue of the discipline of secular law.

Jewish life is governed by a unique legal system. This system covers all civil, secular topics as well as those religious concerns associated with the temple service and Jewish rituals. More accurately stated, there are no exclusively secular matters. All issues of human concern have religious overtones that require evaluation with the yardstick of Torah morals and ethics. Confrontation of our legal system with the "law of the land" is a recorded phenomenon of respect for the legal system of others. The Jew is ordered to respect the alien legal systems of the lands in which he finds himself as sojourner or citizen. This respect for the legal system of our country is in itself an ethical imperative. Our present secular legal code declares the use or possession of various drugs to be in violation of the law. This fact imposes a religious obligation on the Jew to heed the "law of the land." This obligation is further enforced by our sense of appreciation to our own government for the freedom granted us, as citizens, to foster the growth and maturation of the Jewish community in the United States. On this soil we have nurtured a vigorous Torah scholarship, that has invigorated a new genera-tion of Torah committed youth to dedicate themselves to our way of life — a life that is the antithesis of the life style of the drug culture proponents.

D) Group association and identification in the development of an ethical personality.

Man is a social animal. His full maturation is not attained until he interacts with a social group. In this conflict of self-interest, interplay of emotions, and sharing of personal views as to the nature of man in society, the finishing touches are put on the plastic ethical nature with which he was genetically en-dowed. The great concern in Jewish ethical literature with proper choice of friends, neighbors, and even transient associ-ates, is the recognition of this reality of social maturation. The morally repugnant act when seen repetitively becomes less repugnant. In time it becomes possible, then morally in-nocuous, and ultimately even desirable. The socially accept-able becomes personal conduct if not personal ideology.

The procurement of illegal drugs necessitates contact with the morally degraded elements of our society. Even if these drugs were not threats to good health, or in violation of the law of the land, it would be morally abhorrent to interact socially with the merchants who control the sale of these drugs. Mari-juana may not be physiologically more damaging than alcohol, nicotine, or tobacco tars, but its procurement is fraught with unique ethical dangers. Torah ethics accepts a "domino theory" of ethical behavior. Transgression fosters transgression. The only bulwark against immoral conduct is a meticulously presented analysis of the immoral component of every new situation. The selective or relative morality of situation ethics is but a thinly veiled commitment to an amoral view of man's obligations and responsibilities. This meticulous analysis compels the individual to forego the claim to personal immunity, when society as a whole is succumbing to a raging epidemic that is inflaming and decaying the collective soul of our communities. Protective or curative measures must be supported by all. The debate as to whether soft drugs lead to hard drugs is only of academic interest. What is fully documented is that most hard drug users have previously used or concurrently use soft drugs. Both drug classes thus pose ethical dangers to our society and therefore must be viewed as we view other antagonistic elements in our community.

The association of alcoholic beverages with Jewish ritual is to be specially noted. Many have recorded the low incidence of alcoholism among Jews who follow the traditional life style of the Orthodox Jew. Indeed, the place of these beverages in traditional Jewish life when compared to their social niche in secular society may well serve as a foil to develop the fundamental ideological differences between two life styles. "Wine gladdens the heart of man." In Torah life, wine adds a ritual and ceremonial note to raise a repast from a physiological necessity to a uniquely human act of eating. This uniqueness is the concomitant realization that eating is for a special purpose. It is to permit man to function as the paragon of God's creation. It is "eating at God's table" — a concept of sharing (as if possible) with God, responsibility for this complex world that we inhabit.

The failure to realize this dual function of all human physical activity is likened by our Sages to an idolatrous act. The core concept of Judaism is an absolute monotheism. This monotheistic basis denies all dichotomies. The distinction between body and soul, science and religion, holy and secular is useful for pedagogic purposes of classification. It has no validity in our ethical system. Food and drink are therefore associated in Jewish law with multitudes of laws and ritual obligations to inculcate this truth from early childhood. When man divorces this uniquely human, non-physiological, function of nutrition and shares his food needs with the rest of the biotic world, he incurs the special disdain of our Sages. The prodigal son, the drunkard, and the glutton are each viewed as one who has disgraced his human stature, and failed in his obligations to his fellow man.

The Torah-directed life style of the Jew has much to say about the current drug scene. It is critically important that it be said clearly and articulately. If it can be presented to our youth before their minds are so damaged that truth no longer stimulates their ethical nerve fibres, it will be evaluated as one of the alternatives available to them. History compels the optimistic conclusion that, once evaluated, it will be chosen as the only life style fit for man.

XVII. GENETIC ENGINEERING: A COMPOSITE OF ETHICAL PROBLEMS

Genetic engineering is probably the "hottest" topic in medicine today. New advances in medical science have raised many ethical problems. The most crucial of these problems, those that apparently lie in a twilight area, concern themselves with genetic engineering.

My emphasis will be on the current practical problems arising in this area, rather than those that may arise in the foreseeable future which deal with eugenic concerns and the dangers that can result from our assuming mastery over man's genetic pool. Such mastery could lead to two basic applications for genetic engineering. The first is the replacement of defective genes and the second is genetic cloning. The latter falls into the future problem area. It involves the artificial induction of superior beings by controlling fertilization through careful selection of gametes. This is not only a genetic problem, but rather a political-sociological one. Cloning can be even now effectuated by a tyrannical ruler using techniques of human husbandry; i.e., by preventing some groups from procreating while favoring procreation by other groups. While scientific advances may facilitate genetic cloning, it is not needed to achieve success.

What is of current relevance is the problem of defective genes. I will begin my analysis by focusing attention on a small point that has major consequences in this area. The ultimate goal in genetic engineering is of course the replacement of defective genes. We are already able to manipulate the genetic make-up of lower organisms with a certain degree of finesse. Theoretically it should be possible to select a desirable gene and introduce it into an organism that needs it. If a child is born with a bio-chemical deficiency it should be possible to isolate the needed gene from a normal individual and with "viral" microsurgery, using a virus as a carrier, cure the genetic disease. While offspring of the "cured" parent, will nevertheless inherit the diseased gene, they too can be cured in a similar manner as their parents were. Thus, for example, every Tay-Sachs child will be given the genes to make the enzyme, hexosaminodase, the lack of which causes the disease syndrome. This will solve their problem. If things were this simple, most moral people would agree to solve these problems in this convenient manner rather than insisting on the purity of the genetic make up. In actuality, we have done so, for example, in cases of cleft palate, which is a genetic disease that society accepts and is willing to pay a price, for, by allowing birth to take place and then subjecting the child to surgery that is painful, time consuming and costly but which usually will result in an essentially normal functioning indi-vidual. We don't insist on performing amniocentesis during early pregnancy to determine if the child will be born with a cleft palate. While society is willing to carry the burden in such cases for this disease, it is unwilling to do so for other diseases where the child cannot reach maturity. Nor will it do so right now in the case, for example, of hemophilia, where the individ-ual could reach maturity if we would be willing to pay the price in terms of donating enough blood and the cost involved in isolating the factors lacking in the child. Theoretically, with further improvements, hemophiliacs could live a normal life. Indeed because of medical advances many hemophiliacs can reach child bearing age, and thus more of them are being born than ever before. In earlier times no male hemophiliac reached maturity while the female carrier who was not affected by the disease survived and remained part of the genetic pool. There is concern on the part of some, who say that an investment of a few thousand dollars to normalize a cleft palate patient is acceptable but that repeated expenditure of many thousands of dollars for blood fractions to temporarily correct the hemophiliac's disease may not be acceptable. The same can be said about cystic fibrosis. The ultimate goal of genetic engineering is to correct defective genes by a simple method even though the gametes will remain defective. With such a method conceivably all defective gene problems could be resolved.

The potential for genetic engineering implies that it is desirable to institute mass screening of individuals to determine carriers of defective genes. What is the approach to the problem of screening, according to *Das Torah* using Tay-Sachs disease as a case in point?

The first question is: Does the concern itself violate Torah standards? May we worry that the fetus may conceivably be a bearer of Tay-Sachs disease? Are there not areas of knowledge about which we say "That which is hidden don't search?" The Halacha is quite clear on this issue. The Shulchan Aruch (Even Ezer 2:7) says "A man should not marry a woman from a family of "lepers"[1] or epileptics." This implies that one should examine the genetic background of one's spouse's family to insure that one does not marry a genetic "cripple." Thus a "heter" is available to concern oneself with the genetic consequences of a marriage.

The duty to search, question, be concerned, must be evaluated with respect to our ability to handle the consequences of

1. The term used is *metzora*. The exact medical condition is not fully known to us.

this concern. Professor Robert Hook, the distinguished philosopher, posed the question in his lecture before retirement: "Do you believe that knowledge is an absolute good?" The audience naturally responded in the affirmative. He then picked up his roll book and said, "I have next to each person's name the date when they are to die. How many wish to know it?" Only a few responded in the affirmative. He said "You see, knowledge is not an absolute good." Thus, some available knowledge may prove to be detrimental to man's functioning effectively as a human being. There are limitations to the usefulness of total knowledge.

Recent medical reports indicate that 84 (as of August 1977) metabolic diseases are now detectable in cultured fibroblasts, about 30 of which have a ten-fold incidence over Tay-Sachs disease. Should one be checked for all these diseases? If one gets a genetic profile how do we handle this information in terms of our social relations with a prospective mate? As medical science advances, the number of diseases detectable will increase until conceivably most of them can be predetermined. Thus if society has a eugenic concern then we should remove all defective genes, to prevent the birth of a defective child. Are we prepared to live with this knowledge? There are over 3,300 known genetic diseases.

What are the consequences of knowing that one is a Tay-Sachs carrier, as against that of being uninformed. There is a very small chance that one is a carrier and even a smaller one that one's mate is. Even if both are, then there is a 25% chance that the child will be defective. Naturally, 25% is significant and should compel some action.

A letter published in *The New England Journal of Medicine* (v. 292, no. 7, Feb. 1975) by Dr. M.D. Kuhr, a distinguished pediatrician from St. Elizabeth's Medical Center of Dayton, Ohio notes that an Advisory Committee of Physicians in their community opted against the screening program for Tay-Sachs disease based on the fact that assuming a 4% carrier rate, out of 6,000 Ashkenazic Jews in Dayton only two marriages, according to probability, could produce Tay-Sachs children and only one child would probably be born with the disease. To prevent this possibility, 72 individuals would be identified as carriers (heterozygotes). The decision was then made that the psychic burden on the carriers was too high a price to pay for the prevention of a single case. Thus psycho-social consequences or problems of knowledge that cannot be handled, were deemed to outweigh the potential benefit of testing.

Let us examine the problem for its halachic consequences. If one is tested and determines that he or she is a carrier, there is no problem if one's mate is a non-carrier. But how does one handle this information? The social implications are quite obvious. Carriers would be discriminated against in cases even where one's potential mate is a certain non-carrier. Why should one introduce to his family's genetic pool a possible defective gene that would require testing by future generations prior to marriage? Are we to declare all carriers unmarriageable?

There is also great concern for the import of this knowledge on a teenager whose self-image is just being fashioned. It is a time when any "blemish" is magnified to become a psychological stress with unknown consequences. Mass screening in schools, where confidentiality is difficult to maintain, is particularly objectionable. Students, if only frivolously, often reveal intimate details of their family life, since they are unaware of the social consequences.

Of greater significance is the fact that mass screening is objectionable because it creates a mass hysteria that pressures people to undergo testing. The pro-testing group, namely the Tay-Sach's organization, holds a pro-abortion viewpoint. It reassures people that even when both are carriers, the genetic status of the fetus can be determined, and a defective one aborted. However, such an abortion is halachically not permissible. This fetus will be born perfectly normal, and becomes ill only after approximately one year of life. If one advocates destroying this fetus, because ethical-moral considerations define this child as no longer a child after six months of life, must we not then say that a man with only six months to live is no longer a man? How does one distinguish between such an abortion and euthanasia?

The premature termination of life in hopeless cases is not only being advocated, but is being carried out. The push to euthanasia did not begin until the approval of abortion, for it was the next "logical" step. Thus a "domino" effect in ethics exists whereby terminating life prematurely in the fetal stage results in an impetus toward termination prematurely at the other end of the scale. By extension one can justify earlier termination of adult life once it is determined that the individual is useless to society, as is done in an Eskimo society.

To digress for a moment, genetic screening which is the basis of genetic engineering opens up new problems. There are at least ten neoplastic diseases that involve a hereditary predisposition. One example is breast cancer. Should we place a young lady from a family where this disease can be found in the category of a family of "lepers" or "epileptics," to be avoided? Or should we say that the genetic background simply means a higher than normal incidence of this disease requiring one to be more rigorous in taking preventive measures by more frequent and more thorough check-ups. For in this case, unlike with Tay-Sachs, something can be done about it. Thus, the knowledge of the presence of familial breast cancer may be important knowledge and a massive study of the family background may be desirable. Such knowledge has positive rewards.

Returning to the consequences of Tay-Sach's screening. If amniocentesis shows that the fetus has the disease, abortion is a desirable recourse. Yet this procedure is halachically considered murder. In the time of the Sanhedrin a non-Jew would be put to death by *Beth Din* for such an act, while a Jew was subject to death by the Divine Hand. This is because it is felt that man cannot administer a punishment severe enough for such a crime. Only the Almighty can institute the appropriate punishment for a Jew who should be uniquely sensitive to the moral and ethical consequences of his actions.

One can argue that he does gain something from amniocentesis; he determines if the child is normal, and thus avoids a prolonged period of uncertainty. However, amniocentesis is not halachically permissible since there is, in practice no alternative to a positive finding except abortion. Few are those who can withstand the emotional stress resulting from not aborting under these circumstances. Those with strong faith in themselves cannot be certain how they will act when the circumstances become a reality. Our society is no longer constituted to provide emotional support to women in such a predicament, and inevitably abortion will be performed because of the manifest danger to the mother's mental and physical well being that arises. Amniocentesis is not permitted because it is a preliminary to murder and cannot be halachically justified.

For married people, the possible consequences of positive findings for both partners are contraception, sterilization, abortion, divorce, or the risk of having an abnormal child. However, in reality the result inevitably will be amniocentesis and possibly abortion. It is halachically forbidden except to those past child-bearing age who can be tested to determine if their children are homogenous or not.

I wish to conclude with a Midrash from Parshas Kiddoshim (M.R. 24:3). "Rav Brachya in the name of R. Simon said: It once happened that I visited Abba Yossi who was sitting and learning Torah by a spring. A spirit appeared to him, that lived in the spring. He said to him: You know how many years I lived with you in good relations. You come here, your wives, your children come morning and night and I never harmed anyone. You must know that there is an evil spirit that wishes to move in over here who destroys people. Warn the townfolk. Tell them that whoever has a spade, whoever has an ax, whoever has a rake should come here in the morning and look into the water. As soon as you see a turbulence you will beat with your tools and shout We win. We win."

The Midrash Rabba, written by the Tannaim and Amoraim uses such a story to express fundamental truths of Judaism. One can interpret the aforementioned in the light of our awareness that as Jews we live in a state of coexistence with our society until some major event transpires. A "new spirit" enters our society and this spirit is evil for us. What does one do? You can make believe that it will go away and move to a different society. The Midrash tells us we rather should start shouting "we have a better spirit — a better way" and not accept the inevitability of the evil spirit. The new spirit of genetic engineering is on the verge of coming in. If we sit complacently and think it is someone else's problem, then this new spirit will come in and it will be our problem and our children's problem and it will do us evil. However, we are convinced that we have something to offer. "Our spirit," our way of doing things, applies to everything including the problems of medical ethics. If we create situations where we allow questionable programs to be carried out under the aegis of Torah institutions like mass Tay-Sachs screening, then the implication exists that mass screening of married couples elsewhere and amniocentesis and abortion are acceptable. If we let it happen then it is our fault and they win. If we do not let it happen, then we will surely win.[2]

TESHUVAH REGARDING TAY-SACHS SCREENING

Rav Joseph Ekstein
Director
Dor Yeshorim
198 Keap Street
Brooklyn, NY 11211

Dear Rav Ekstein, shlit"a

As per your request, I am recording my observations concerning the Dor Yeshorim Tay-Sachs Screening Program. As you know, my father-in-law, Hagaon Moshe Feinstein, ztzq"l opposed the mass screening program administered by the National Tay-Sachs organization — for three reasons. First, an accurate understanding of genetic inheritance is not shared by all. Many are likely to equate the recessive gene carrier with a disease

2. The above criticism of mass testing has led to the organization of a well-managed program (Dor Yeshorim) which guarantees confidentiality and does not reveal test results except in response to a *dual* request for assurance that at least one of the coded identification numbers is not a carrier. Only when both I.D. numbers are carriers will the response be "not compatible."

carrier who is to be shunned or placed under social sanction with respect to *shidduchim*. Mass screening increases the possibility that confidentiality may be unwittingly breached, or even frivolously, by the one identified as a carrier who is unaware of the social implications.

Second, the psychotrauma of a positive finding on a teenager, whose self-image and self-esteem is still being developed, can be quite harmful. Indeed, testing of those not of marriageable age is hardly justifiable.

Finally, the involvement of a secular organization in the screening and essential follow-up counselling of detected carriers poses a threat to the maintenance of the religious standards that guide the Orthodox Jewish family. Amniocentesis and abortion, contraception and sterilization are the standard alternatives offered during genetic counselling. These alternatives are not usually available to those whose lives are governed by halachic norms. We must solve our problems within the framework of halachic Judaism. Counselling must sensitively reflect the halachic guidelines that restrict the options available to the family.

It is therefore a source of personal pride and appreciation that my father-in-law's ztzq"l halachic concerns convinced you and your colleagues to design an effective screening program for our communities that obviates the halachic objections. My compliments to you; may the many tragedies your program will prevent be merited to you as the *mitzva* of *pikuach nefesh*.

XVIII. THE LIVING WILL OR NATURAL DEATH LAWS: AN HALACHIC ANALYSIS

The withdrawal of life-support systems from terminally ill patients has been given legal approval in the California Natural Death Act of 1976. Similar bills based on the patient's legal right to instruct his physician concerning the use of life-sustaining treatments are now pending in New York and New Jersey. The latter state, long in the limelight on this issue because of the Quinlan case, adopted in January 1977, a system based on the recommendations of a "prognosis committee," whereby a decision to cease all support systems can be made in the absence of patient directives. These bills and guidelines make ethical and legal assumptions to validate their conclusions. What are these ethical assumptions and what validity do they have when evaluated by the objective yardstick of Torah ethics?

1) *Assumption One:* There is a "natural" limit to human life other than death. The "artificial" prolongation of human life beyond these limits by means of modern medical technology is neither necessary nor desirable.

Evaluation: There is validity to the assumption that medical intervention be limited to life prolongation and not death postponement. But can anyone draw sharp lines of demarcation between the two clinical states? How terminal must the patient be before he is really terminal? When is it "unnecessary" or "not beneficial" to the patient (viz. sec 7186)? If we are committed to the fundamental concept of the infinite worth of human life, then a piece of infinity is infinity! Excluding the very problem of "triage" or the finite resources of society, there is no patient-oriented reason other than *Assumption Two* to differentiate between the care to be given the terminally ill patient and that given the one with cure prognosis.

2) *Assumption Two:* Such artificial prolongation can cause unnecessary pain and loss of patient dignity.

Evaluation: "Dying with dignity" is an ill-conceived slogan, nothing more. Death with dignity is the end result of a dignified life style. In itself, death is a truly undignified behavior. If those attending the dying patient behave in sensitive, dignified fashion, no indignity other than that of death itself is involved.

A treatment modality that prolongs or accentuates pain without hope of cure is indeed to be questioned on ethical, moral grounds. If the patient chooses to continue treatment, despite the discomfort it causes or prolongs, he is entitled to the full support of the health profession. If he requests the discontinuance of therapy, emphasizing his inability to cope with his pain-filled existence, the absence of any real hope for cure makes this request binding on all who minister to him. (Talmudic precedent can be found in *Avoda Zara* 18a. See also *Ketuboth* 104a).

Obviously this consideration is valid only in the conscious patient, not in the patient in deep coma. Such a patient is a burden on others but not to himself. The decision to withdraw life-support mechanisms can only be made by equating terminal illness with death; the imminent with the actual. What dangers lurk in such an assumption! Can active euthanasia be far behind?

Living wills set a dangerous ethical precedent

3) *Assumption Three:* Adult persons have the fundamental right to control decisions relating to their own medical care.

Evaluation: Does such a right exist? I think not! The right to suicide or even self-mutilation is denied to an individual in all ethical systems associated with the dominant religions of Western civilization. As discussed in *Assumption Two,* pain — physical or psychic — may be a significant factor in permitting passive self-euthanasia by the conscious terminal patient, but this is not relevant to the comatose patient. This denial of the right of self-destruction has been extended by case law, to compel blood transfusions even when the patient's refusal was based on religious principles. The living will thus has little ethical validity in the absence of intractable pain or when the patient is in coma.

4) *General concerns:* The scale-up from personal ethics to social legislation introduces many new concerns that require careful evaluation.

A) *The domino theory* in social ethics: Living will legislation may bring active euthanasia a step closer to social acceptance, just as abortion legislation has made passive euthanasia legislation more palatable.

B) *The confidence quotient:* The bill specifies that the attending physician or any employee of the health facility caring for the patient cannot witness the living will. Why? The courts fear that unscrupulous, mercenary interests may endanger the life of the patient. How sure can we be that the terminal illness diagnosis and prognosis be free of all taint of personal advantage and is truly altruistic?

C) *Ethical aesthetics:* Is there a proper claim on the finite resources of our society and its medical community when life support mechanisms are being maintained without hope of cure? Surely such a claim is valid in a society rich enough to spend massive sums on nonsense fads, commercial sports, or highway beautification programs. Must highway aesthetics be given priority over ethical aesthetics? If continuation of life support systems after the point of no return, will emphasize our commitments to the infinite worth of man and prevent the callus that forms on the soul when a "plug is pulled," it is money well spent. God forbid, that we ever reach the time when true triage must be practiced, with "God committees" deciding who gets the respirator or kidney dialysis equipment and lives, and who dies.

Torah ethics boasts of 3500 years of testing and confirming its validity as a code of conduct fit for man created in God's image. Its evaluation may well serve the needs of all who make up the complex mix of American society.

Halachic Responsum Sent to *Raphael Society* of the Association of Orthodox Jewish Scientists, December 5737.

XIX. THE BASIC QUESTIONS — PURITY OF HEART AND MIND

Note: The following article originated as a response to a series of questions posed by the editor of *Commentary.* It was first published as part of the "Commentary Symposium on the State of Jewish Belief" in August, 1966, and subsequently in book form by Macmillan.

THE QUESTIONS

1. In what sense do you believe the Torah to be divine revelation? Are all 613 commandments equally binding on the believing Jew? If not, how is he to decide which to observe? What status would you accord to ritual commandments lacking in ethical or doctrinal content (e.g., the prohibition against clothing made of linen and wool)?

2. In what sense do you believe that the Jews are the chosen people of God? How do you answer the charge that this doctrine is the model from which various theories of national and racial superiority have been derived?

3. Is Judaism the one true religion, or is it one of several true religions? Does Judaism still have something distinctive — as it once had monotheism — to contribute to the world? In the ethical sphere, the sphere of ben adam la-chavero, what distinguishes the believing Jew from the believing Christian, Moslem, or Buddhist — or, for that matter, from the unbelieving Jew and the secular humanist?

4. Does Judaism as a religion entail any particular political viewpoint? Can a man be a good Jew and yet, say, support racial segregation? Can a man be a good Jew and be a Communist? A Fascist?

5. Does the so-called "God is irrelevant" question, which has been agitating Christian theologians, have any bearing on Jewish thought or belief? What aspects of modern thought do you think pose the most serious challenge to Jewish belief?

M.D. Tendler: Avtalyon says: Sages, be most careful in your teachings...lest your students who succeed you, drink thereof and die — and thus the name of God be profaned" (B. Avot I).

The errorless transmission of the truths of our faith requires meticulous care in choice of words and idioms. The personal *rebbe-talmid* relationship is the main guarantee that errors due to faulty student comprehension do not blemish the perfection of the Torah concept.

This attempt to state some of the most fundamental beliefs of Judaism through the impersonal medium of a published article is fraught with danger. The written word lies naked on the page with all its inadequacies exposed for all to see. Can I possibly prevent the false impression, the mistaken connotation, the erroneous deduction, in this attempt to teach the Torah "while standing on one foot"? Unfortunately, I cannot hope for such perfection of idiom. I can, however, beseech the reader of my words to remember that my inadequacies are not those of our Torah whose words are "absolute truth complementing each other in their righteousness" (Psalms 19:10).

(1) The literal interpretation of the theological doctrine of divine revelation differentiates Torah Judaism from the organized faith communities that have arisen as deviants from the traditional form. The development of Christianity during the last 1900 years, and the development of Reform and Conservative Judaism during the last hundred years, represent similar deviations from the literal interpretation and application of the divinely revealed code of human conduct — the prophecy of Moses: the Torah.

It is the foundation of our faith that God spoke unto Moses as a teacher instructs his pupil. Unlike other prophets, Moses did not receive his instructions while asleep or in a trancelike, physiologically abnormal state. Moses heard and recorded the word of God while mentally alert and intellectually responsive. Only Moses received a Torah, a code of human conduct. The later prophets did not simplify or "liberalize" the Torah. Their sole contribution was to instruct the Jewish nation and to exhort them to observe the Torah without modification. This prophecy, the Torah, was received by Moses accompanied by the necessary explanatory details. The actual words and sentence structure of this divine revelation are recorded in the Pentateuch — the Five Books of Moses.

There is yet another record of divine revelation — the oral tradition, comprising the explanatory notes and details of the biblical ordinances recorded in the Pentateuch. The oral tradition is now recorded in the Talmud along with the later man-made rabbinic edicts. Thus the Pentateuch and the oral tradition are of equal authority, are equally obligatory on all Jews as the direct instructions of God to His nation, Israel.

The Torah (written and oral) records our duties at times in great specific detail, at other times in broad principles. The Talmud presents for study the differing opinions of our sages with respect to the application of these principles to specific legal or ritual circumstances. These discussions, pro and con, enable us to encompass intellectually the full intent of the God-given principle and thus give us the understanding to apply it to new situations not discussed in the Talmud. Thus, in this age of scientific, technological, and sociological advances, the divinely revealed Torah principles serve as the objective yard-sticks by which all new concepts and actions are measured. The vital and vibrant biblical scholarship of the Orthodox communities in all the countries of the diaspora, as recorded in the staggering number of *responsa* publications dealing with every aspect of human endeavor, bears irrefutable testimony to the greatness of our Torah. Rather than stultifying and mummifying our lives by lists of obligations and prohibitions, our Torah, as given to us by God on Mount Sinai 3300 years ago, has proven applicable to all societies throughout our nation's history.

The vast majority of these applications of Torah principles has been codified in our law books — the writings of the *Geonim*, *Rishonim* and later sages. These applications serve as precedents, simplifying our task of applying the Torah principles to modern-day problems. These secondary sources have, through centuries of usage, been accorded the greatest allegiance by the Torah community. The renown of the Shulchan Arukh, authored by Rabbi Joseph Karo, earned for it the role of final arbiter in all disputed matters upon which he commented.

The role of the rabbis as lawgivers must also be mentioned. We are careful to distinguish between the divinely revealed oral tradition recorded in the Talmud and the later man-made edicts. The rabbinic edicts were mostly designed to protect the biblical law — to serve as "fences around the law." For example, the present-day observance of dietary laws necessitates the use of separate dinnerware for meat and dairy meals. This is a result of a rabbinic injunction proclaimed to protect the biblical law against cooking mixtures of meat and dairy products. When, in response to the religious needs of our people, the rabbis promulgated new laws and edicts, occasionally unrelated to biblical ordinances, these rabbinic laws became obligatory on every Jew after they proved themselves useful and practicable. The Bible specifically sanctions the rabbinic right to make such ordinances. Thus in actual practice, every traditional Jew accepts these rabbinic laws as no less obligatory than the biblical laws.

All the biblical commandments are binding on every Jewish male when he reaches thirteen years of age. Women, who assume their religious obligations a year earlier, are exempt from some of the 248 positive commandments. Likewise, those commandments specifically ordained for the *Kohen* or Levite apply only to these classes of Israelites. There are no significant distinctions between the sexes with respect to the obligation to abstain from the 365 biblical prohibitions.

Because of the destruction of our Temple and the exile of the Jewish nation from the land of Israel, many of the commandments governing the Temple service and priestly conduct are not in effect today. Only 77 of the 248 positive commandments and 194 of the 365 biblical prohibitions play any significant role in the conduct of the Jew living outside of the land of Israel. The others await the coming of the Messiah and the re-establishment of the theocracy in Israel.

All the Torah commandments are given to the Jew for his ennoblement. There are none "lacking ethical or doctrinal content." The *mishpatim* are those commandments whose purpose and utility are clearly understood. The *hukim* are those whose full intent is not known. It is axiomatic that our omniscient God did not give us arbitrary or purposeless responsibilities. All of them have ethical or doctrinal import. King Solomon boasted that he knew the true reason for the *hukim* of the Torah except those governing the sacrifice of the red heifer (Numbers 19:1-13). Our failure to devote adequate time and effort to the study of our Torah has drawn a veil over some of God's commandments.

Throughout the ages, the dictum, "The study of the Torah equals all else," has encouraged our rabbis to search for and to postulate reasons even for the *hukim*. The dangers that are inherent in this search are obvious. A human reason for a divine edict may be in error. The refutation of this man-given explanation can weaken the integrity of the biblical commandment in the mind of the uncritical layman. A prime example of this pattern is the health-code explanation for the Jewish dietary laws offered by the early writers of Reform Judaism. To many laymen who accepted this explanation as the true one, the efforts of the U.S. Department of Agriculture and the Public Health Service exempted them from the obligation to observe these tenets of our faith. Thus the search for reasons (*taamei hamitzvot*) has been rejected by some of our scholars as unnecessary, if not essentially destructive. However, to many of our sages, exercising their right and responsibility to search for new insights as valid reasons for all Torah commandments best fulfills their obligation "to teach them diligently to thy sons" (Deut. 6:7).

The specific example of the questioner concerning the prohibition of wearing clothing woven of a mixture of wool and linen fibers is explained by Maimonides (in his *Guide of the Perplexed*, 38) as a denial of idolatrous practice and a reaffirmation of our monotheistic belief. In his study of the idolatrous religions that were once the dominant cultures, Maimonides noted that the priests wore, as a talisman, clothing of wool and linen while holding in their hands a mineral object. The symbolic intent was to encompass the entire material world during their idolatrous service and thus invoke the blessings of the many gods on the main industries of man: agriculture (linen), animal husbandry (wool), and mining (mineral).

This reason of Maimonides is meaningful to me in 1966 C.E. Even my garments proclaim the oneness of God! However, the key reservation must be understood. Maimonides discerned this reason through his intense study of our Torah and his understanding of the secular world of his day. If he be proven totally in error, the Torah commandment against the wearing of clothing woven of wool and linen threads (*shatnez*) is in no way either less binding or less acceptable to us.

(2) There are two aspects of Israel's unique status as the chosen people. The first and foremost is the fact that the nation Israel chose to accept the Torah way of life. The Talmud is careful to point out that the same choice was offered to all other nations of the earth. Only Israel agreed to accept the discipline of the 613 commandments. To this day, any convert to Judaism joins in this "chosenness" by dint of voluntary choice. No Semite was ever given the choice to become an "Aryan" by the racists who undertook to destroy the chosen people.

Does the fact that Israel is the chosen people demean other peoples who have not chosen to follow the Torah way of life? No one even casually conversant with biblical and talmudic literature can doubt that this superiority is uniquely different from the chauvinism and racism abounding in the secular world. It is — and this is the second aspect — a uniqueness of responsibility, an assumption of obligations that casts no aspersions on those who chose not to assume them. It is the divine scheme for humanity that only if the Jew observes his Torah, and the non-Jew his Torah, will the world survive. If there is synergistic benefit in this association, it is as it should be.

The Talmud sums it up most beautifully (Talmud Bavli, Berakhot 17a). The wise men of Yavneh were the chosen of the chosen. The nation Israel had just suffered the near-fatal blow of the destruction of the Temple and the desolation of the land of Israel. In the hands of the wise men of Yavneh rested the destiny of the nation Israel. Never before had any group more reason to feel superior. Never before had the crown of Israel, the Torah, become the sole property of so few. Yet "they were wont to say, 'I am but one of God's creatures just as is my unlearned friend. My labors are in the city, his in the fields. I arise early to my work just as he does. Lest you say I accomplish much and he but little, note. Whether much or little, it is all the same if one but intends to do his work in the name of Heaven.' "

(3) Judaism is a world religion. It is not a compilation of local tribal customs. It speaks to Jew and non-Jew. It is a Torah — a code of conduct for all humanity. It is the only "true" religion.

God promulgated different obligatory behavior for Jew and non-Jew, just as He differentiated between man and woman, and between *Kohen*, Levite, and Israelite. The seven Noahide laws are binding on all humanity. They have served as the basis for all civilized codes of conduct. They are the Torah of the non-Jew. In this sense there is but one true religion. There is one true record of the responsibilities demanded by God of man created in His image.

The concept of a "true religion" is often intertwined with the requirements for "salvation." The 613 mitzvos are the means by which a Jew earns salvation. The non-Jew can achieve the same goal in seven giant steps, the Noahide laws. If the non-Jew observes these fundamental laws, his religion is equally true.

Despite the influence Judaism wielded in forming most of our present concepts of man-God and man-man relationships, it still remains basically unique and distinctive. The broad brush strokes on the canvas of all the great religions testify to their Judaic heritage. The fine art work bears little resemblance. Even the concept of one God, monotheism, is not equally shared by Judaism and Christianity. The total negation of the "other gods" is found only in Judaism. Negation of intermediaries in prayer to God, denial of all superstitions and astrological influences as opposed to the conscious will of God, is the basic tenet only of Judaism. The monotheistic belief in a personal God who knows and cares, who ordains and instructs man even in every mundane human activity, evolved in a practical, not theoretical, code of conduct only in Judaism.

Our greatest "contributions" to humanity have yet to be taken over by other religions. For example, let us analyze the Sabbath concept in Judaism. Its socio-economic value has been properly recognized. However, in the Age of Man, this contribution fades in significance when compared to the main concept of the unique Jewish Sabbath. It is a day reserved for vigorous toil in the uniquely human sphere and for a rebalancing of the spiritual and material influences on man. For six days we share with the beasts of the field a common goal — material sustenance. Only on the Sabbath day, when we proclaim God the Creator and man as one created in His image, do we assume truly human proportion. To rest by lying on a hammock, ruminating on a large meal, would be a further mimicry of the animal world. To "rest" by spending the day in intellectual disquietude, by mind-wracking study of God and man, by fatiguing examination of the children's studies that week, is a uniquely Jewish concept hardly understood, let alone shared, by other religions. The manifold Sabbath prohibitions that serve to negate man's role as a creator in opposition to God, coupled with the obligation to make of the Sabbath meal and dress as occasion for material pleasure, serve to establish the golden mean for every Jew. God decries both asceticism and hedonism. He has given us a way of life fit for mortals who aspire to human existence.

Similarly, in the ethical sphere of man-man relations, Judaism remains unique despite the espousing of the Judaic heritage by other ethical systems. Our Torah stands on the two legs of man-man and man-God relationships. Our system of ethics cannot be "taught on one foot" because it is the intertwining of the man-God relationship that guarantees the appreciation of the Torah concept of ethics. The famous response of the Great Sage of Israel, Hillel, to the request of the non-Jew that he teach him our Torah while "standing on one foot" best summarizes this thesis. Indeed, it can be summarized by the simple dictum, "that which is hateful to thee do not do unto your fellow man," but the understanding of this dictum requires you "to go and finish your studies of the man-God relationship."

Empathy, charity, kindness are the results of observance of the Torah commandments governing our mutual responsibilities. They are not the motivations of these observances. I feed the poor because the Torah so ordained. This permits me to absorb in my personality both sympathy and understanding for the needs of others. If my feeding of the poor depended upon the pre-existence of a sympathetic soul, as presumed by ethical systems without religion or by those of other religions, the poor would all too often go hungry if I were not at that moment emotionally attuned.

In most ethical concepts, our differences with other religions far exceed the similarities. Indeed, we have much to contribute to all nations. The lack is only that of suitable and articulate exponents to serve as "prophet unto the nations."

(4) Judaism is a total code of conduct. No sphere of human endeavor is neglected. Most certainly there is the "opinion of Torah" (*da'at ha-Torah*) on the great political, sociological, and economic issues of the day. A Jew cannot observe our Torah commandments and at the same time be a Communist, or a racist, or a Fascist, any more than he could at the same time be a Shintoist or Buddhist. The Torah governs how much profit he may make on a sale, as well as how much charity he must or may give. The law of the land is given Torah support to make it binding on every Jew — but only if it does not require the Jew to violate the ethical teachings of his religion. If men band together to establish a democratic welfare state, or a monarchy, the Torah then adds its authority to the need for observance of all the laws of the kingdom. If, however, taxation is imposed inequitably; if the integrity and worth of the individual are denied; if due process of law is violated, the Torah cries out with divine authority — "Cease and desist, lest I turn the world to ashes!" A racist doctrine, promulgated by the governmental authorities, is as hateful to the Jewish citizen as the promulgation of the classical anti-Semitic ordinances so familiar to the Jew of history.

(5) Our living God becomes irrelevant only when we, while proclaiming Him Creator on Friday eve and declaring Him King on Rosh Hashanah, interpret Psalms 115:16 all too literally: *the heaven is the Lord's* — but *the earth He gave unto man*. That is a "God is irrelevant" theology. By reciting at Kiddush Friday eve

that God redeemed us from Egypt — in addition to making the heavens and the earth, we proclaim that "the God of Israel liveth forever." It is when we believe that God is too exalted to care about man's daily activities that He becomes irrelevant. When we believe that God is too generous to restrict man by the issuance of a code of human conduct similar to the laws he proclaimed to the rest of creation does He become irrelevant.

When a Jew discusses the great problems of our age — race relations, population control, international problems — from a purely sociological, political or economic point of view, he proclaims that the God of Judaism is irrelevant. The Torah *does* have a point of view. The Torah is a repository of solutions to the problems of mankind that are both progressive and feasible. We dare not overlook them. The Living God speaks anew to us each day. Would that we listened.

The great challenge to Torah Judaism has always been the same. Ignorance of the teachings of our faith is our only worthy adversary. Appreciation of the relevance of Torah concepts is directly related to the time devoted to the study of our Torah teachings. Ignorance of what we say and what we believe can mislead our youth into assuming that the Torah does not maintain its role of guide and mentor of human conduct. With man appearing more and more in the central role of master of the physical universe, the omnipresent danger of declaring man as creator and master assumes new proportions.

The invasion of the uniquely human area, that of memory, intellect, and emotion, by psychotropic pharmaceuticals which put the veneer of mechanistic behavior on this last vestige of uniquely human attributes, points up most sharply the need for a Torah system of human values. The Jew recites each morning in his prayers, "Although the preeminence of man over beast is naught ... we, the children of Thy covenant can truly say 'How goodly is our lot, how beautiful our heritage.' "

XX. THE HALACHIC STATUS OF THE SWORDFISH
TO REMOVE A STUMBLINGBLOCK — A TESHUVA
WITH AN EPILOGUE

In March of 1966 (5726), I issued a fact sheet to be distributed to the many people who called my office at Yeshiva University requesting information on the kashrus of swordfish (*xiphias gladius*). The essential paragraph reads as follows:

The adult forms sold commercially fail to evidence a single scale. A number of ichthyologists have reported that the swordfish does have scales when born and loses them during maturation. All evidence, however, points to the probability that these scales, if they ARE present, are not of the kosher variety.

Recently, the Conservative Rabbinical Assembly declared swordfish to be a kosher fish, and disseminated this opinion widely, creating doubt and confusion even among Torah-observant Jews.

The following analysis of the halachic and scientific literature is presented to reaffirm the practice of centuries during which the swordfish was not eaten by Jews who believed in the Divine origin of Torah and the authority of our Sages.
> These you may eat of the fishes,
> all that have fins and scales.
> — Leviticus: 11. 9-12

Rashi defines the Biblical term "scale" (*kaskeses*), in accord with Nida 51b, and Chulin 59a and 61b, as an outer layer (shell or peel) set in the skin of the fish resembling the armor (coat of mail) worn by Goliath when he fought with David (viz., Targum —*kalfin*). The *Tosefos* commentary emphasizes that the exact definition of the term *kaskeses* was handed down in errorless transmission as it was given to Moses on Mount Sinai.

The Ramban's definition of the term *kaskeses* has served as the primary source for all the leading Torah scholars whose rulings have determined Torah law and custom. The following is a free translation of the halachic definition of that type of scale which serves to identify the fish as a kosher variety:

Do not think that the term scale refers to those structures that are set into the skin and actually affixed to it. Rather it refers to a type of structure like the nail of man which can be removed from the skin of the fish by hand or with a knife. But if it be affixed to the skin and not separated therefrom at all (i.e., no free margins), then the bearer of these scales may not be eaten. This is the intent of the Talmud in referring to the scales as an outer garment that can be peeled off as one peels a fruit or removes bark from a tree. It resembles the overlapping scales of armor designed to guard the gaps in the armor plate lest a thin arrow get through.

The *Shulchan Aruch* (Rama) records this definition as halachically binding, and no halachic authority has ever disputed this definition. The biological term "scale" includes such skin structures as occur on the tail of the rat. Removeability is not a prerequisite.

With this definition in mind, it must be obvious that the biological term "scale" is not the same as the Torah's definition of *kaskeses*. Ichthyologists recognize four types of fish scale. The *ganoid* scale found on the sturgeon, or the *placoid* scale of the shark are specifically excluded from the Biblical term *kaskeses* since they are not "removable" scales. Indeed, the educated layman would not see any similarity between the heavy bony plates of the sturgeon or the needle-like projections on the shark skin and the classic kosher scale of the whitefish or carp.

During the last few decades, sturgeon was sporadically classified as a kosher fish by some who were ignorant of either the halachic or the scientific facts. Despite the absence of any "scales" that could be seen and removed; despite the confluence of so many auxilliary signs considered by Talmudic authorities to be typical of non-kosher fishes such as a ventral mouth, black roe, a heterocerclic tail (divided into unequal halves), many Jews had been misled into a violation of a Biblical ordinance. Contributing to the confusion was a Fisheries Leaflet (No. 531) of the United States Department of the Interior, prepared by I. Ginsburg, Systematic Zoologist on the staff of the Fish and Wildlife Service. This leaflet was issued in response to many inquiries "whether certain fishes are kosher." Despite the author's lack of halachic qualifications, and despite many inclusions that clearly mark this leaflet as a biological treatise unrelated to the requirements of Torah law, this leaflet has once again appeared to mislead and misdirect Jews anxious to observe Torah law. It serves as the main proof cited by the Conservative clergy for the kashrus of swordfish. In their 1966 *Proceedings*, they cite:

1. The *Talmudical Encyclopedia*, which notes in the caption under the drawing of a swordfish that it has "scales as a juvenile but not when mature." No decision is rendered in that article on the halachic status of the swordfish. Instead the caption refers the reader to the text material in which the swordfish (*akaspatias*) is listed among those fishes who lose their scales upon capture. Any unbiased reader would have concluded that the "swordfish" of this article is not our *xiphias* species;

2. A citation from the *Darkai Teshuva* (quoting the *Keneses Hagedola*) that is customary to eat the "fish with the sword" because although it appears to have no scales, it sheds its scales while battling to resist capture;

3. A reference to an article published in *Hapardes* that proposes swordfish to be a kosher fish;

4. A statement by a Dr. Ganz that Dr. Bruce B. Collette of the United States Department of the Interior is a competent ichthyologist. This is preparatory to a statement that Dr. Collett confirms the competence of Isaac Ginsburg who issued the government leaflet. A literature citation from *Nakamura, et al.* (1951) that swordfish have scales as juveniles completes the "halachic" treatise.

Now the facts—halachic and scientific:

1. Not one of these references cited refers to the removability of the scales — an absolute requirement for a kosher scale;

2. The fishery leaflet lists *eels*, *catfish*, and *sharks* as fish that have scales and therefore are kosher — as "kosher" as sword-

fish. The *Talmudical Encyclopedia* lists these unequivocally as NOT kosher. Clearly the scale of Ginsburg is NOT the scale of Leviticus! The *Talmudical Encyclopedia* does NOT list the swordfish as kosher. The kosher fishes are so captioned and they include tuna, bonito, mackeral, sardines, hake, carp, and sunfish.

3. Even Ginsburg clearly sounds a warning with regard to swordfish. "Swordfish during early juvenile stage of life have scales that are markedly specialized and rather unique. They are in the form of *bony tubercules* or expanded compressed platelike bodies. These scales are rough, having spinous projections at the surface and they do not overlap one another as scales in most other fishes do. With growth the scales disappear and the larger fish *including those sold in the market have no scales.*" Yet they cite the *Darkai Teshuva* who clearly refers to a fish possessing scales as an adult. The citation, which they quote only in part, concludes (in free translation): "A government official questioned my teacher as to the kashrus of the 'fish-with-the-sword' since it has no scales. My teacher therefore took a black cloth, placed it in the net, and proved that the fish does shed its scales, confirming the truth and accuracy of our Torah laws." All ichthyologists deny that the swordfish has scales as an adult.

4. *Nakamura* (p. 269) claims that in the 454 mm size (20 inches) scales are already degenerate. They appear clearly as "bony plates" only on specimens up to a size of 8 inches — hardly the ferocious fish of the *Darkai Teshuva* citation. Surely the swordfish of America is not the fish referred to in the *Keneses Hagedola!*

5. Rav Z. Waltner, Rosh Yeshiva of the Ets Haim Yeshiva in Tangiers, writes that the swordfish is commonly sold in his area. When he arrived in Tangiers 16 years ago, he determined that the great rabbinic authorities of the Sephardic world such as the author of *Vayomer Yitzchak*, as well as the famous Rav Itzel of Ponovitz, identified this fish as non-kosher. However, several families ate this fish claiming that they have been taught that the swordfish "sheds its scales during its anger." Rav

Waltner asserts, "I investigated the matter with the fishermen who unanimously agreed that they never found any scales on the fish, net, or its immediate vicinity."

6. Dr. G. Testa of the Institute for Marine Science in Monaco — a world renowned marine biologist — writes:

"L'Espadon...ne possede pas de'ecaille. La peau est lisse chez les adultes, mais chez les jeunes elle est couvert de petites tubercules." (Translation): "The swordfish does *not* have scales. The skin of the adult is smooth but the juvenile forms are covered with small tubercules." The term "tubercules" is used to indicate a variation in skin texture as contrasted with a true scale.

7. Dr. James W. Atz of the Museum of Natural History in New York clarified the literature reference for me in an interview on April 5, 1968. I quote from our conversation: "The scale of the swordfish is so atypical that it cannot be considered as the usual scale."..."It is not a true scale but a spiny process."

8. F.R. LaMonte,* curator emeritus, Department of Ichthyology of the American Museum of Natural History, reported in 1958 on the "keeled" scales of the swordfish to which *Arata* (1954) and *Nakamura* (1951) make reference, and which serves as the basis of Dr. Bruce Collette's statement that swordfish have scales. *(Bulletin, American Museum of Natural History*, Vol. 114, article 5, page 391, 1958.) I quote verbatim:

They resemble in general, the placoid scale originating in the dermis (under the skin not on top of it) with its spine eventually breaking through the epidermis. — [The placoid scale is found on the shark] — (see diagram from *Arata, G.F.*)

9. There is a teshuva from a recognized halachic authority (*Shemesh Tzedaka, Yoreh Deah*, 14) concerning spinous scales: "that which appears as scales are not true scales for they

---

*Miss LaMonte also reports on a new type of scale, found on some specimens which she calls a "glassy scale." In a lengthy telephone conversation with Dr. LaMonte on April 9, 1968, I was unable to clarify the exact nature of this scale (unreported by any other investigator). Dr. LaMonte asserted that, "It does not resemble any other known scale and therefore cannot be classified as one of the four scale types."

resemble nails and are but stiff dermal projections...the fish is therefore *not* kosher."

10. The reference to the *Hapardes* article ignored my own point-by-point rebuttal of this article in the following issue as well as other rebuttals that were subsequently published.

11. Since Dr. Collette's opinion in the mainstay of the responsum published by the Rabbinical Assembly, I wrote to Dr. Collette on April 1, 1968 to evoke from him a clear statement concerning the nature of this swordfish scale. The question I posed read as follows:

"Does the scale of the juvenile swordfish resemble the scale of the whitefish or carp with respect to its relatively loose attachment to the underlying integument?"

I received the following response dated April 15: "Specifically the scales of the juvenile swordfish *do not* resemble the scale of whitefish or carp in respect to their loose attachment to the skin. However, they are certainly homologous to scales of other fishes." (The term homologous is defined as "showing a similarity of structure, embryonic development and relationship." For example, the hand of man and the wing of the bat are homologous structures.)

This recent clarification by Dr. Collette should be recognized even by the author of the spurious *heter* as a total refutation of the scientific basis for their conclusions.

The Talmud lists but two exceptions to the absolute requirements of having visible scales:

a) Fish that shed their scales when netted, like the mackerel;

b) Fish that have scales developing later in the life cycle; consequently the juvenile forms that lack scales may be eaten since they *do* have scales at maturity.

But no place in the Talmud or the responsa literature is there any reference to such a deviant: a fish that has scales as a juvenile but not as an adult. Yet the Conservative clergy must be aware of Talmudical references to some form of swordfish since it is mentioned in the *Talmudical Encyclopedia* article that they cite as a basis for their *heter*. If the swordfish of the Talmud had "juvenile scales," the Talmud would have surely recorded this fact.

I discussed the above presented facts with my great teachers,* Rav Moshe Feinstein, my father-in-law זצוק״ל ויבל״ח and
Rav Yosef Dov Soloveitchik, שליט״א and they concur with my
decision that on the basis of the evidence presented, the swordfish (xiphias gladius) is a non-kosher fish.

May those who observe the laws of the forbidden and the
permitted merit joining in the feast of the Leviathan.

BIBLIOGRAPHY OF SCIENTIFIC LITERATURE

Arata, George F., 1954 — "A contribution to the life history of the swordfish
    Xiphias gladius Linnaeus." Bulletin of Marine Science of the Gulf &
    Caribbean, Vol. 4, No. 3, pp. 183-243.

Ginsburg, Isaac, 1961 — "Food fishes with fins and scales." Fishery leaflet No.
    531, U.S. Dept. of Interior, Fish & Wildlife Service, Bureau of Commercial
    Fisheries, Wash., D.C.

LaMonte, F.R. et al., 1958 — "On the Biology of the Atlantic Marlins, Makaira
    Ampla (Poey) and Makaira Albida (Poey). Bulletin of the American Mu-
    seum of Natural History, Vol. 114, Art. 5, pp. 377-415.

LaMonte, F.R. and Marcy, 1941 — "Ichthyological Contributions." Internation-
    al Game Fish Association, Vol. 1, No. 2.

Nakamura et al., 1951 — "Notes on the life-history of the swordfish Viphias
    gladius Linnaeus." Japanese Journal of Ichthyology, Vol. 1, No. 4, pp.
    264-271.

XXI. THE SWORDFISH AND THE SWORD OF
KING CHEZKIYAHU
AN EPILOGUE TO A TESHUVA

When our love was great we shared the edge of a sword, now a
bed of 60 cubits does not suffice.

— Sanhedrin 7a

While in the library of the Museum of Natural History, studying the available source material for the foregoing teshuva, I felt
a sense of foreboding.

Are we entering a new era of open aggression — of overt hostility — in our relationships with Conservative Judaism?

Is there to be a new battlefield, another "mechitza"-issue which will further divide the small remnant of Israel?

Must I accept it as tragic reality that the mechitza, the halachic wall that divides the Torah-observant Jew from the adherents to Conservative Judaism, has made of us two religions?

Judaism has been decimated during these last three decades by two destructive forces — physical destruction in Europe and spiritual destruction in Europe and America. Conservatism has legitimatized desecration of our Shabbos, killed by neglect our marital laws, and destroyed the sanctity of family life and natural heritage by their failure to consistently enforce the divorce laws and the laws governing conversion to Judaism. Are they now intent on doing away with the dietary laws by planned confusion so as to salve the conscience of their adherents who don't observe these laws anyway?

What motivated them to issue a "heter" on swordfish? Do they believe that the Jewish lust for swordfish steak must be satiated so as to guarantee the progressive development of Jewish consciousness and Torah observances? Since they try to maintain a "Torah-true" posture why the "big-lie" technique? Why do they quote the Ramban's definition of a scale (kaskeses) and then cite a series of secular references none of which comment on the prime requisite of a kosher scale — its removability? Why, if they accept the Ginsburg leaflet as adequate halachic precedent, did they not permit eel, shark and catfish? Did they decide on the basis of consumer surveys that a "heter" on swordfish and sturgeon is commercially more significant and therefore give it priority? Why the conscious premediated attempt to pervert the truths of our Torah concerning Shabbos, Taharas Hamishpacha, divorce and marriage laws? — and now sturgeon and swordfish?

How clearly I hear the echo of our silence! Why have we been so diplomatically obtruse in our reaction to Conservativism? Why do I evoke shock and disbelief in the sixty-five-year-old *stalwart of a Conservative Temple when I tell him that his spiritual leaders do not believe that God gave us our Torah; or when I tell him that his "rabbi" does not have smicha, or even familiarity with any of the texts that have traditionally been identified with rabbinic scholarship?*

We should have demanded of the Conservative laity, during these many years, a defense of their observance of Simchas Torah. Why do you dance with our Torah? Since your "teacher and preacher in Israel" maintains that this Torah was "written by a group of wise men over several centuries and fraudulently presented as the actual word of Hashem," why do you embrace, kiss this symbol of deceit? Why not substitute your son's text in nuclear physics or molecular biology? Why not go way out and design the Torah crown in the shape of the double helix of the DNA molecule?

No! I am not prepared to "drum out" of our small army of survivors the millions of non-observant Jews. Amoral leaders who sold their Torah birthright for a bowl of lentil soup, cannot be permitted to lay claim to the blessing of Isaac and thus mislead and misdirect. They must be forced into a full disclosure of their ideology and theology. Let their adherents know where they are being lead. If you want to go about composing responsa in imitation of the rabbis of Israel, let me first see some statistics. How many of your congregants have kosher homes but trefa stomachs because of a double standard that exempts the Chinese restaurant from halachic disciplines? How many of the children of your members keep kosher homes? When did you exhort your women to go to mikveh? How many of your second- and third-generation Conservatives are liberal enough to have married outside the faith? What is your honest prognosis for your fourth and fifth and *fiftieth* generations? Will they be recognizable as sons of Abraham or will they be indistinguishable from the rest of humanity, or inhumanity? A moratorium on lies — a designation of several years as "years of integrity" — will give us the opportunity to win back the Torah allegiance of all Israel. Judaism can survive if we have masses of non-religious, non-observant Jews. Judaism cannot survive the hyphenation of "Conservative," "Reform," and "Reconstructionist."

* * *

What did King Chezkiyahu do? He plunged a sword into the entrance-way to the study-hall and announced: "He who refuses to involve himself in the study of our Torah [la'asok ba'Torah] let him be pierced with the sword." They searched from Don to Beersheva and could not find man, woman, or child who had not mastered the laws of the holy and the defiled, the permitted and the forbidden (Sanhedrin 94b).

King Chezkiyahu did not demand *limud Ha'Torah* study alone, but *la'asok Ba'Torah* — personal involvement with Torah as a way of life, a fact of Jewish existence, not a transient phase of our national development. The first Torah blessing recited by the Jew every morning reads:

Blessed are you Hashem who has sanctified us by commanding us la'asok ba'Torah!

Torah study is not an exercise in medieval Jewish literature or ancient legal codes. Our Oral Torah is not "one man's opinion" to be disputed by every theology student with twelve credits in Old Testament literature. It is our way of life, our source of truth, our reason for existence as a unique entity among the nations of the world! You can't pervert Torah truths without incurring my resentment. You cannot deny this perversion without incurring my disdain. If you would but state your position with integrity, with candor, you would not threaten the spiritual well being of my children; we could then devote our energies to the task of returning the wayward, of convincing those who err of their error. Let us meet your laity if you dare! Let the truths of our Torah — without "apologetica," modification, and explanation — be spoken. Never after will they be able to accept the half-truths and whole lies of the clergy of Conservative Judaism. Don't threaten my right to my heritage, my Torah. Write your own Torah! Find your own prophets! Originate your own customs! — Don't plagiarize my ideas, my literature.

*   *   *

When our love was strong, when all Jews knew their obligation and were cognizant of their failings, we were governed by the laws of friendship and brotherhood: — chastise your friend; — do not hate your brother in your heart.

The strong helped the weak and then was helped in turn. No matter how tight the situation, even on the edge of a sword, our love for each other — tzadik and sinner — governed our daily lives.

But when the source of this love is rejected, when God and His Torah are equated with "God concepts," "constructs," and "ethical theories," the sword must be turned into a scalpel to cut away the diseased tissues lest the whole body of Judaism grow weak and die. When our brethren substitute the Decalogue alone for the entire Dialogue of *"Peh el Peh adabair bo"* — the dialogue between Hashem and Moshe which gave to man his code of conduct, and to the Jew *his* code of conduct — they substitute partial "truth" for the absolute truth of our Torah. Even the vastness of the Universe is too small to contain truth and falsehood. Let those who sought strength for their failings by organizing a union of non-believers once again become the lonely in search of truth, in quest of that code of conduct that is "goodly in the eyes of God and man."

XXII. EVOLUTION, A THEORY THAT FAILED TO EVOLVE: UPDATE FOR TORAH SCHOOLS 5748

I. In January 1982 (McLean vs. Arkansas Board of Education 5 January 1982) the Arkansas Board of Education was enjoined from requiring all its schools to teach creation-science along with the theory of evolution. The main thrust of the legal decision was that "creation-science with its belief in *creatio ex nihilo* based on the first eleven chapters of the book of Genesis is unquestionably a statement of religion ... assuming for the purposes of argument, however, that evolution is a religion or religious tenet, the remedy is to stop the teaching of evolution, not establish another religion in opposition to it."

On March 4, 1987, the U.S. Supreme Court declared unconstitutional a Louisiana law requiring that creationism be taught along with evolution in the public schools.

II. Is the theory of evolution "secular humanism" or is it the consequence of scientific methodology?

How should this theory, once again a source of ferment and controversy in educational and legal circles, be taught in our Yeshivot and Day Schools whose students' first exposure is to the creationism of *sefer Beraishit?*

I believe it to be a categorical imperative of Torah education that teach we must! We cannot ignore the ferment nor deny the massive influence of the theory on the thought processes of our society because:

a) "Razor-blade" textbook revisions will not cure the focal infection of doubt that the theory inoculates when presented as a religion of secular humanism. Removing the offending pages from the textbook, no matter how carefully it is done, denigrates the power of Torah truths to compete in the arena of ideas and ideals — an arena in which we have never lost a match despite an occasional loss of a round!

b) Evolutionary theory is all pervasive in our culture. Can we hide all the "restorations" of dinosaurs found in our museums and publications? Must we draw in *yarmulkas* and *peyot* on all artist renditions of prehistoric man? Even if our students are not yet questioning the "first eleven chapters" of *Sefer Beraishit*, we have the obligation of *at petach lo* to initiate the questioning lest the questions burst forth when we, the teachers of Torah truths, will not be there to provide the answers to satisfy the mind and soul of the questioner.

c) We are obligated to teach the truths of *Hashem's* interaction with the natural world.

שבת ע״ה. — אמר ר׳ שמעון בן פזי א״ר יהושע בן לוי משום בר קפרא כל

היודע לחשב בתקופות ומזלות ואינו חושב — עליו הכתוב אומר „ואת פעל ד' לא
יביטו ומעשה ידיו לא יראו" (ישעי' ה, י"ב). . .

א"ר יוחנן מנין שמצוה על האדם לחשב תקופות ומזלות שנאמר (דברים ד, ו)
„ושמרתם ועשיתם כי היא חכמתכם ובינתכם לעיני העמים" איזו חכמה ובינה שהיא
לעיני העמים? זה חישוב תקופות ומזלות.

. . . . to refuse to master the science of astronomy is to refuse to see *Hashem* as He interacts with the natural world. Rav Yochanan added it is a *mitzvah* to do so because it fulfills the commandment of *Hashem* to study and apply Torah knowledge. This is the wisdom and the understanding that the other nations appreciate.

III. The Theory of Evolution: in search of scientific facts.

Much has happened to the theory since it was formulated by evolutionists in the late 1800s. Darwinian evolution was quickly rejected when the science of genetics burst forth on the world of science. Darwin's lack of knowledge of genetics allowed him to propose erroneous mechanisms of evolution such as: inheritance of acquired characteristics (Lamarkian Inheritance) and the blending of inherited characteristics rather than their discreet segregation and independent transmission to the new generation. His reliance on stress as a main evolutionary force and his preoccupation with the negative consequences of inbreeding were quickly rejected by the neo-Darwinists. The Synthetic theory was substituted. This theory incorporated the new science of genetics and introduced the influence of chance mutations and the "DNA story," to bolster the faltering theory. The basic construct remained the same: "Life having appeared once upon the earth, the various species have arisen one from the other by a gradual process of modification extended through untold generations." The mechanisms of evolution continued to elude the scientific search. "Facts" were accumulated based on:

- the fossil record;
- the resemblance of organs between disparate species (homologous organs);

- the purported presence of vestigial organs in "higher" species;
- evidence from comparative biochemistry, immunology, and embryology;
- evidence from artificial selection during animal husbandry and from the "green revolution."

The latter, an application of genetic principles to plant crops, has given us an era of worldwide food surpluses, and has defused, forever more, the demographic time bomb erroneously proposed by Malthus.

Thomas H. Huxley, the great publicist of Darwinian evolution, restated the basic construct as follows: "All species have been produced by the development of varieties from common stocks; by the conversion of these, first into permanent races, then into species by the process of natural selection essentially identical with the artificial selection by which man has originated the races of domestic animals."

Is there any evidence that such has occurred in nature without the intervention of man? Until a mechanism can be proposed that will enable us to produce such "races" under scientifically controlled conditions, the evolutionary theory remains but a theory, and one under severe attack from its former proponents.

Gradualism, as proposed by Darwin, failed to explain species development. No organism becomes more fit for survival with one miraculous modification called a mutation. The light sensitive eye is advantageous to the organism, but not the colored spot on the arm of a starfish from which it is supposed to have evolved. Why would a starfish with a small red birthmark be selected for survival? ... A limb for locomotion is an asset, but not a bump on the streamline shape of an eel-like creature from which it is supposed to have evolved ... Why were these "sports" or misfits saved for survival? Or by whom? Such concerns are summed up in a poem printed in many biology texts entitled "Ode to a Starfish" with a refrain of "Some call it evolution and others call it God!" The so-called "proofs" of evolution are mere records of biological phenomena or areas yet uncharted by scientific methodology.

Our sages who were "observant" Jews par excellence, were fully aware of homologous organs and even relied on this knowledge to set halakhic directives.

"An epidemic of intestinal disease amongst pigs requires a declaration of a day of fasting because their intestinal tract resembles that of humans."   שו"ע או"ח תענית תקע"ה, ג

"Vestigial organs" most often reflect our ignorance rather than our investigative skills. The thymus gland, now known to be a major component of our immune system, was once listed as a vestigial organ. The appendix, the classic vestigial organ is now suspected of playing a role in immune mechanisms as well.

IV. The theory collapses

The forty-year dominance of the modern synthesis ended in Chicago in 1980 at the conference simply entitled "Macroevolution." Gradualism, the basic tenet of evolutionary theory was rejected on the basis of its former greatest proof — the fossil record. The summation of the participants, all leading evolutionists, reads like an epitaph on the tombstone of the modern synthesis née Darwinism. Evolution, according to a near unanimous reanalysis of all available data, does not move at a stately pace with small changes accumulating over periods of many millions of years. The principal feature of individual species within the fossil record is stasis, not change. The record, read without bias, reveals that species remained unchanged and then suddenly disappeared to be replaced by substantially different but related species. There are no transitional forms! All have been postulated to complete the record but they do not exist except in the imagination of the evolutionists. New terms have been coined to define the fossil record as it is, not as evolutionists wish it would be! Punctuated equilibrium, episodic evolution is now the master. "The Omnipotent position of adaptationism embodied in the Modern Synthesis is overturned."[1]

1. *Science* v. 210, 21 November 1980 p. 883-866.

The concurrence of three leading evolutionists in a review of the *Evolutionary Synthesis: Perspectives on the Unification of Biology*, edited by Ernest Mays and William B. Provine, is the summation of the theory that was.[2] Niles Eldridge, the reviewer, states: "I think that the idiosyncracies of these major individuals are underplayed. A case can be made that individuals, rather than disciplines, were responsible for the emergence of the synthesis and its particular character...Why....did so many biologists accept the synthesis though it remained unproven? I suggest that this is all the explanation we need: the persuasiveness of a few highly talented biologists, promulgating a single simple and rationally very appealing set of ideas."

There is no theory of evolution to attack or defend in 1987. There are stirrings of a new modification of the theory that must now begin to search for new "proofs." The theory is too appealing to let die. Like the Bohr atom, it may not be true but it helps the human mind to grapple with the massed data from the biotic world. It allows for some order in the chaotic profusion of genera and species.

Indeed we owe Darwin, despite the erroneous views he held and the short lived theory he proposed, a great debt of gratitude. The idea of studying animal disease models to find cures for human ills would be an irrational pursuit, were it not for the educative impact of evolutionary doctrines. Metabolic pathways ellucidated in bacteria are assumed to be imitative of human metabolism, thanks to Darwin and Huxley.

V. What are the religious/halakhic problems posed by the theory? There are but two. One is inherent in the theory — the age of the universe measured in billions of years, not 5748 as recorded on our calendars. The other is randomness or undirected evolution that denies existence of a creator. This is not a component of the theory but an atheistic stance of some evolutionists. The belief of many evolutionists is that there are constraints on evolutionary expression that do not permit random evolution. How far is the concept of restraint from that of *Adon Olam*? If it is professed that the hand of God guided the

2. *Science*, April 1981.

evolutionary process, we can affirm Darwin's statement in a
letter to the author John Fordyce who wrote *Aspects of Skepti-
cism*. "It seems absurd," he wrote on May 7, 1879, "to doubt that
man may be an ardent theist and an evolutionist?"

What about the age of the earth and the claims of man's
descent from other species and other variants of humanity?

The Torah view of *motar haadam min habehaimah ayin*,
"there is little difference between man and animal," is a goad to
man to rise from animal to human life by dint of our exercise of
Free Will to accept Torah instructions in developing our life
style. The church, in deifying a man, opposed the notion that
man was but another animal in God's biblical zoo. The *gedolei
hador* at the time of Darwin found little to criticize in the theory
or its scientific findings. The *Tifereth Yisroel*, whose masterful
commentary on the *mishnayot* is the "standard in the field,"
published his *Drush Ohr HaChayim* in 1842. This was, coinci-
dentally, the year the Piltdown man (later found to be a hoax)
was discovered. The *Drush* is found (regrettably few find it!) in
the back of the first part of *seder nezikin* of the "big" *mishnayot, Yakhin Boaz*. In this treatise, he relates to the Darwinian
evolutionary theory of his time as follows:

„ועתה אחי ידידי ראו. . . כי הסוד הזה שנמסר לאבותינו ורבותינו והם גלוהו לנו
זה כמה מאות שנים מצאנוהו שוב בהטבע ברורה לעינינו בזמנים המאוחרים כבזמנינו
הבהירה ביותר"

He relates to the fossil finds in the Carpathians, Himalayas
and in the "Mountains of Cardillan in America" and describes
the fossil remains in each stratum. He refers to the Mastadon
found in Siberia, and to flesh eating "inguanadons" and her-
biverous "megalasourus."

מכל האמור נראה ברור שכל מה שמסרו לנו המקובלים זה כמה מאות שנים
שכבר היה עולם פעם אחת ושוב נחרב וחזר ונתקיים זה ארבע פעמים. . . הכל התברר
עכשיו בזמנינו באמת וצדק. . . ולפענ"ד שאותן בני אדם שהיו בעולם שנקראין
פראאדעמיטען ר"ל הבני אדם שהיו בעולם קודם בריאת אדם הראשון העכשווי, הן הן
974 דורות שנזכרו בשבת דף פ"ח וחגיגה דף י"ד שהיו נבראים קודם בריאת העולם
העתיי.

Neither the age of the earth, the fossil finds of strange creatures nor the evolution of man, posed any "threat" to Torah truths as understood by the *Tifereth Yisroel*. Indeed, data from carbon dating lead/uranium, and other radioactive time clocks affirm the great age of the earth. It is difficult to accept the explanation of some "literalists" amongst our rabbinic leaders who see the irrefuted facts of science as a test of man's faith. The Creator purposely placed dinosaur bones, and other fossil remains where we would find them to test our faith in the teachings of our Sages. As we see, one of our great Sages taught us otherwise. The concept of a "testing" God with a flair for the dramatic, is also foreign to Torah theology (except in the "testing" of Abraham).

Did Hashem make this last world in six days and rest on the seventh, or was it six millennia? Either assumption can be correct. What is not an assumption but an axiom of our faith in Hashem, is that the Creator of the world revealed Himself to Adam and Eve and taught them the truths of the man-God relationship. These truths were transmitted to Noah and then to Shem who, as King of Jerusalem, Malki Tzedek, met with Abraham and refined the truths that Abraham evolved from his own study of the God-nature relationship. Shem's daughter Tamar married Judah, the son of Yaacov, and gave rise to the Kingship of David and Moshiach.

This evolution of man is what is relevant to our lives in the service of Hashem. The Torah is not a biology text nor even a book of history. It is an instructional book of morals and ethics for Jew and non-Jew. All other lessons learned therefrom may or may not be the true intent of our God who ordered every word of our Torah to be inscribed by Moshe the great-grand-nephew of Judah.

VI. To sum up: In 1987 there is not one piece of scientific evidence for macroevolution or the development of one species from another. All our work in genetics, molecular biology, recombinant DNA explains variations within the species but does not offer any mechanism for the development of new species. Ye the notion of a common thread that interconnects the biotic world is both utilitarian and elegant. It does not violate any Torah beliefs. The Talmudic literature refers to prior worlds and earlier men before the present world that is dated 5748 years from the birth of Adam and his wife Eve. Some of our great Torah sages accept this literally and see in it a concurrence with the scientific claim for a very ancient world. No one dare label such a belief heretical, even if personal family tradition is to accept that the world was created *ex nihilo* 5748 years ago.

The key to presenting the above discussion to students is to do so without apologetica. If our Torah traditions were in full opposition to scientific claims, we would not hestitate to reject the relative truths of science in favor of the absolute truths of our Torah. But if it is possible, through intensive study of both Torah and scientific texts, to avoid such confrontations it is our duty to do so. There can not be real conflict between Torah and Science, only apparent disagreement.

The *Elokim* who created the world in accord with *His* laws of nature came down on Mt. Sinai to give us the Torah, and announced to all creation *Anokhie Hashem Elokekha* I am the *Hashem*, the personal God who designed a Torah for you and I am also *Elokekha*, your God who put into effect all the laws of nature.

XXIII. AN EPILOGUE

מילחא כי סריא במאי מלחי להו?

אמר להו בסילתא דכידניתא

ומי איכא סילתא לכודניתא?

ומילחא מי סריי?

The wise men of Athens posed a riddle to Rav Yehoshua Ben Chananya: "When salt rots how do you preserve it?"

Rav Yehoshua answered: "With the afterbirth (placenta) of a mule."

The Athenians were taken aback. The result of a cross between a horse and a donkey, the mule, for all its virtues, is a sterile freak of nature. "Where can you find a placenta of a mule?"

Rav Yehoshua responded, "Does salt ever rot?"

(Tractate Bechorot 8b)

The riddle and its solution represent a conflict of ideologies. The wise men of Athens challenged Rav Yehoshua to accept reality! The Torah, the salt that preserved the Jewish people throughout their tortuous history is no longer viable! In the age of Hellenism, the Torah cannot compete. Your salt is rotting, they claimed! Rav Yehoshua responded to the critical intent of their argument. Surely you don't mean to propose that we give up Judaism. Your armies, your executions, famine and pestilence failed to cower us. No sophistry could hope to succeed. Obviously you are suggesting that we invigorate Judaism with an admixture of Hellenism; that we modernize antiquated Torah life with a veneer of modernity. Let us see how this works out in the laws of nature. Admixtures are often quite impressive. A fusion of horse and donkey chromosomes results in a new breed of animal — the mule — with many advantages over both horse and donkey. But the mule has one biological defect. It is a sterile freak of nature. It cannot give rise to a second generation!

Indeed, we can modernize Torah law by deletion and subtraction. We can emphasize the great truths of Judaism and discard the minutiae of Halacha that encompass every moment of our life — day and night. We can even expect noticeable successes. Synagogues will increase their membership. More children will attend religious schools. There may even be a rebirth of active observance of aspects of Sabbath and holidays.

But if we made these changes by fusing Torah concepts and practices with concepts and practices of other ethical systems, we will have made a philosophical and theological mule. The result will be a sterile generation that will not give rise to another generation of Torah-loving Jews.

Does salt ever rot? Does Torah, the words of timeless God, ever become antiquated? Our life style may indeed be changeless in a world of constant flux, not because it is antiquated, but because it needs no change.

Torah laws may appear somewhat cumbersome in detail. There are many who appreciate the fundamental ethical concepts upon which these laws are based, but who balk at the rigid details of the day-to-day observances. Bear in mind that our Torah speaks the language of eternity. Broad principles can give rise to one generation, but no more. They are infertile, sterile concepts unless they are vitalized and made virile by the uniquely Jewish preoccupation with the details of moral behavior. The laws of our Torah are the salt that preserves the Jewish family, so that Torah values can be perpetuated from generation to generation.